ADULT ONLY
JOKES

COLLECTOR'S EDITION

HB
HINKLER
BOOKS

Published by Hinkler Books Pty Ltd
45–55 Fairchild Street
Heatherton Victoria 3202 Australia
www.hinklerbooks.com

Jokes and images compiled by Nick Bryant
Cover Design: Mandi Cole
Prepress: Graphic Print Group
Typesetting: Macmillan Publishing Solutions
All images © Getty Images, except image on page 141, © Dreamstime

4 6 8 10 9 7 5 3
10 12 14 13 11

ISBN: 978 1 7418 5855 6

Printed and bound in China

CONTENTS

INTRODUCTION

In this day and age, it's common practice for books to have lengthy introductions in which the author, editor or compiler explain the motivation behind the contents. But this is a joke book for goodness sake. And whether you've bought, borrowed or pinched this book, you really only want to read the jokes. So let's get on with it.

AND SO, TO THE BEGINNING...

A father asks his nine-year-old son, Johnny, if he knows about the birds and the bees.

'I don't want to know,' Johnny says, bursting into tears. Confused, the father asks Johnny what is wrong.

'Oh Daddy,' Johnny sobs. 'At age six I got the "there's no Santa" speech. At age seven I got the "there's no Easter bunny" speech. Then at age eight you hit me with the "there's no tooth fairy" speech! If you're going to tell me now that grown-ups don't really screw, I've got nothing left to live for.'

One day in the Garden of Eden, Eve calls out to God, 'Lord, I have a problem!'

'What's the problem, Eve?'

'Lord, I know you've created me and have provided this beautiful garden and all of these wonderful animals, and that hilarious comedic snake, but I'm just not happy.'

'Why is that, Eve?' comes the reply from above.

'Lord, I am lonely. And I'm sick to death of apples.'

'Well, Eve, in that case, I have a solution. I shall create a man for you.'

'What's a "man", Lord?'

'This man will be a flawed creature, with aggressive tendencies, an enormous ego and an inability to empathise or listen to you properly. All in all, he'll give you a hard time. But, he'll be bigger, faster and more muscular than you. He'll also need your advice to think properly. He'll be really good at fighting and kicking a ball about, hunting fleet-footed ruminants, and not altogether bad in the sack.'

'Sounds great,' says Eve, with an ironically raised eyebrow.

'What's the catch, Lord?'

'Well, you can have him on one condition.'

'What's that, Lord?'

'You'll have to let him believe that I made him first.'

Father O'Malley, the new priest, is nervous about hearing confessions, so he asks the older priest to sit in on his sessions. The new priest hears a couple of confessions, and then the old priest asks him to step out of the confessional for a few suggestions.

The old priest suggests, 'Cross you arms over your chest, and rub your chin with one hand.'

The new priest tries this and achieves a concerned, thoughtful look.

The old priest says, 'Good. Now try saying things like, "I see, yes, go on, I understand" and "how did you feel about that?" alright?'

The new priest tries saying those things and sounds caring and compassionate.

The old priest says, 'Wonderful! Now, don't you think that's a little better than slapping your knee and saying "No shit? What happened next?"'

The good Lord decided to make a companion for Adam. He summoned St Peter to his side.

'My dear Peter,' he said. 'I have a little job for you. I want you to make a being who is similar to man, yet different, and one who can offer man comfort, companionship and pleasure. I will call this being "woman".'

So St Peter set about creating a being who was similar to man, yet was different in ways that would be appealing, and that could provide physical pleasure to man. When St Peter had finished creating this woman, he summoned the Lord to look at his work.

'Ah, St Peter, once again you have done an excellent job,' said the Lord.

'Thank You, O Great One,' replied St Peter. 'I am now ready to provide the brain, nerve endings and senses to this being, this woman. However, I require your assistance on this matter, O Lord.'

'You shall make her brain, slightly smaller, yet more intuitive, more feeling, more compassionate, and more adaptable than man's,' said the Lord.

'What about the nerve endings?' said St Peter. 'How many will I put in her hands?'

'How many did we put in Adam?' asked the Lord.

'Two hundred, O Mighty One,' replied St Peter.

'Then we shall do the same for this woman,' said the Lord.

'And how many nerve endings shall we put in her feet?' enquired St Peter.

'How many did we put in Adam?' asked the Lord.

'Seventy five, O Mighty One,' replied St Peter.

'Do the same for woman,' said the Lord.

'OK. And how many nerve endings should we put in woman's genitals?' inquired St Peter.

'How many did we put in Adam?'

'Four hundred and twenty, O Mighty One,' replied St Peter.

'Do the same for woman,' said the Lord. 'Actually, no wait. I've changed my mind. Give her 10,000. I want her to scream my name out loud when she's enjoying herself!'

AT THE BAR

There's a bar on the rooftop of a tall building in a large city. In this bar, a man is drinking heavily. He asks the bartender for a shot of tequila, then walks out to the balcony and jumps off. Minutes later, he comes out of the elevator and repeats the whole process. Another guy in the bar watches this happen a number of times until curiosity gets the better of him.

He goes up to the jumping man and asks, 'Excuse me, I've noticed that you keep drinking, then jumping off the balcony. And then, a few minutes later, you come back again. How do you do it?'

'Well, the shot of tequila provides such incredible buoyancy that when I am falling and I am about to hit the ground, I slow down and land gently. It's really fun. You should try it.'

The guy, who is quite drunk, thinks to himself, 'Hey, why not give it a shot?'

So he goes to the bar, drinks a shot of tequila, then jumps off the balcony. A splat is heard as he hits the ground.

The bartender looks at the first guy and says, 'Geez, you're an arsehole when you're drunk, Superman.'

Three mice are sitting at a bar in a pretty rough neighbourhood late at night, trying to impress each other with how tough they are.

The first mouse sinks a shot of Scotch, slams the glass onto the bar, turns to the second mouse and says, 'When I see a mousetrap, I lie on my back and set it off with my foot. When the bar comes down, I catch it in my teeth, bench press it twenty times to work up an appetite, and then make off with the cheese.'

The second mouse orders up two shots of sour mash, sinks them both, slams each glass onto the bar, turns to the first mouse, and replies, 'Yeah, well when I see rat poison, I collect as much as I can, take it home, grind it up to a powder, and add it to my coffee each morning so I can get a good buzz going for the rest of the day.'

The first mouse and the second mouse then turn to the third mouse. The third mouse lets out a long sigh and says to the first two, 'I don't have time for this bullshit. I gotta go home and screw the cat.'

A sexy woman in a bar walks up to the counter and motions the bartender over. She starts to run her fingers through his hair and asks to speak to the manager.

The bartender says, 'He isn't here but I can do anything the manager can do for you.'

By this time the woman is running her fingers down his face and into his mouth and is letting him suck on her fingers. She says, 'You're sure he isn't here?'

The bartender says, 'Yes, I'm very sure.'

The woman says, 'Well, I just wanted to tell him there's no toilet paper or soap in the women's toilet.'

A man is sitting outside a bar enjoying a quiet drink when a nun starts lecturing him on the evils of alcohol.

'How do you know alcohol is evil?' asks the man. 'Have you ever tasted it?'

'Of course not,' answers the nun.

'Then let me buy you a drink and, afterwards, if you still believe that it's evil, I promise I'll never touch another drop.'

'But I can't possibly be seen to be drinking,' says the nun.

'Right. Well, I'll get the bartender to put it in a teacup for you.'

The man goes inside and asks for a beer and a vodka.

'And would you mind putting the vodka in a teacup?'

'Oh no,' says the bartender. 'It's not that bloody nun again, is it?'

A drunk rolls into a bar, but the bartender refuses to serve him. 'You've had too much to drink,' he says. 'I'm not serving you.'

Five minutes later, the drunk comes in again. The bartender stands firm.

'There's no way I'm serving you more alcohol. You've had more than enough already.'

Five minutes later, the doors open and the drunk lurches in once more.

'Look,' says the bartender, 'I'm not serving you. You're too drunk.'

The drunk nods. 'I guess I must be,' he says. 'This is the third place in a row that's refused to serve me.'

Four guys are in a bar telling stories. One of them goes to the bathroom and the other three keep talking.

The first guy says, 'I was worried that my son would be a loser because he started out washing cars for a local dealership.

But then they made him a salesman, and he sold so many cars that he actually bought the dealership. Now, he's so successful that he just gave his best friend a new Mercedes for his birthday!'

The second man pipes up, 'I was worried about my son too, because he started out raking leaves for a real estate agent. But then they made him a salesman, and he eventually bought the real estate business. Now, he's so successful that he just gave his best friend a new house for his birthday!'

The third man says, 'Well, my son started out sweeping floors in a stockbroking firm. And now, he's so rich that he just gave his best friend a million dollars in stock for his birthday!'

The fourth man comes back from the toilet. The first three explain that they are telling stories about their sons, so he says, 'Well, I have to admit that my son's story is a bit different. He started out as a hairdresser and is still a hairdresser after fifteen years. And actually, I just found out that he's gay and has several boyfriends. But I try to look on the bright side – it was his birthday last week and his boyfriends bought him a Mercedes, a house, and a million in stock.'

A man walks into a bar with a dog. He puts the dog on the bar and says to the bartender, 'This is the smartest dog in the world. I bet you $5 that he can answer any question you ask him.'

The bartender agrees and asks the dog, 'What's the cube root of 81?'

'Three,' the dog answers immediately.

'That's amazing,' says the bartender, handing over $5.

At this point, the dog owner has to go to the toilet. He asks the barman to look after the dog, and puts the $5 in the dog's collar.

While the man is in the toilet, the barman says to the dog, 'If you're so smart, go down the road and get me a newspaper.'

So the dog leaves. When the man comes out of the toilet he goes ballistic.

'Where's my dog?' he shouts.

The barman calms the man down and tells him about the newspaper. The man immediately leaves the bar to search for his dog. He eventually finds the dog in an alley, screwing a poodle.

'What are you doing?' the man shouts. 'You've never done this before!'

'I've never had $5 before either.'

A bar has a sign up that reads Pianist Wanted. So this guy walks in and tells the owner that he's a great pianist.

The owner tells the pianist to play a couple of songs and if he's as good as he claims, then the job is his. So the pianist sits down and plays a song that nearly has the owner in tears.

'What a beautiful song! What's it called?' the owner asks.

'It's called, "The dog's shagging the cat and my wife's doin' my brother".'

'Um, well, how about playing one more tune.'

So the man plays another tune and this time the manager does break down in tears.

'What do you call that song?' he asks, wiping his eyes.

'The elephant's taking a shit while the lion's licking his balls.'

The bar owner tells the pianist that he has the job on one condition. He must not tell the customers the names of the songs he is playing. So the pianist starts playing that night.

After every song he gets a standing ovation. After about two hours of solid playing, he announces he is going to have a break. He goes to the toilet to take a piss.

On his way out a man passing says, 'Hey mate, do you know your fly's undone and your cock's hanging out?'

'Of course I know it. I wrote it!'

A confident man walks into a bar and takes a seat next to a very attractive woman. He gives her a quick glance, then looks down at his watch for a moment.

The woman notices this and asks, 'Is your date running late?'

'No,' he replies. 'I just bought this state-of-the-art watch and I was testing it.'

'A state-of-the-art watch? What's so special about it?'

'It uses alpha waves to telepathically talk to me,' he explains.

'What's it telling you now?'

'Well, it says you're not wearing any panties.'

The woman giggles and replies, 'Well it must be broken because I am wearing panties!'

The man explains, 'Damn thing must be an hour fast.'

A guy is sitting at a bar, drunk and miserable because his wife just kicked him out and told him never to return. An attractive woman sits beside him. She orders a drink. She looks as depressed as he does.

'Are you alright?' he asks her.

'My husband just left me. He said I was too kinky.'

The guy's face brightens.

'What a coincidence. My wife just kicked me out because I was too kinky!'

This gives the woman an idea. 'Hey, why don't we go back to my place and get kinky together?'

'Sounds perfect,' the guy replies.

When they arrive at her flat, she tells him to make himself comfortable while she gets changed.

The woman goes to her room and takes off her clothes. She puts on a leather g-string, a leather bra, black fishnet stockings, a little leather cap and above-the-knee black boots. She gets out her whip and goes to join the guy in the living room.

She finds him putting his coat on and heading for the door.

'Where are you going?' she asks. 'I thought we were going to get kinky together.'

The guy replies, 'I screwed your dog and shat in your purse, how much kinkier can I get?'

A struggling bar owner decides that he needs a gimmick to bring more people into his bar. After wracking his brains, he comes up with the idea of holding a competition to find the toughest man in town. He puts up posters around town and advertises in the local newspaper.

On the appointed day, his bar is full. The first contestant is a huge man, holding a snapping turtle. The man jumps up on the bar, unzips his pants and whips out his large penis. The man then picks up the snapping turtle and holds it right in front of his dick. With unbelieving eyes, the onlookers gasp as the turtle bites down on the man's penis.

The big man lets go of the turtle and starts swaying his body. The turtle bounces from side to side off the man's hips. After about thirty seconds of this, the man pokes the turtle in the eyes, and the turtle drops to the floor.

'Now,' shouts the big guy. 'Is there another son of a bitch in here that thinks he is tough enough to do that?'

A timid hand at the back of the bar is raised, 'I'll do it, if you promise not to poke me in the eyes.'

A huge muscular man walks into a bar and orders a beer. The bartender hands him the beer and says, 'You know, I'm not gay but I want to compliment you on your physique, it really is phenomenal! I have a question though, why is your head so small?'

The big guy nods slowly. He's obviously fielded this question many times.

'One day,' he begins, 'I was hunting when I got lost in the woods. I heard someone crying for help and finally realised that it was coming from a frog sitting next to a stream. So I picked up the frog and it said, "Kiss me. Kiss me and I will turn into a genie and grant you three wishes." So I looked around to make sure I was alone and gave the frog a kiss. Suddenly, the frog turned into a beautiful, voluptuous, naked woman.

'She said, "You now have three wishes."

'I looked down at my scrawny body and said, "I want an amazing and muscular body."

'She nodded, whispered a spell, and abracadabra there I was, so huge that I burst out of my clothes and was standing there naked.

'She then asked, "What will be your second wish?"

'I looked hungrily at her beautiful body and replied, "I want to make sensuous love with you here by this stream."

'She nodded, lay down, and beckoned to me. We then made love for hours!

'Later, as we lay there next to each other, sweating from our glorious lovemaking, she whispered into my ear, "You know, you do have one more wish. What will it be?"

'I looked at her and replied, "How about a little head?"…'

A bear walks into a bar. He goes up to the barman and says, 'Can I have a large gin and………tonic please?'

The barman replies, 'Sure, but what's with the big pause?'

'Hey, I'm a bear,' says the bear, holding his palms up.

The bar was getting ready to close, so Malcolm asks the nearest woman, 'What would you say to a little oral activity?'

'That all depends,' she responds. 'Your face or mine?'

A drunk gets up from the bar and heads for the bathroom. A few minutes later, a loud, blood-curdling scream is heard coming from the bathroom. A few minutes later, another loud scream reverberates throughout the bar. The bartender goes to the bathroom to investigate why the drunk is screaming.

'What's all the screaming about in there?' he says. 'You're scaring my customers!'

'I'm just sitting here on the toilet and every time I flush something comes up and squeezes the hell out of my balls!'

With that, the bartender opens the door, looks in and says, 'You idiot. You're sitting on the mop bucket.'

A businessman enters a tavern, sits down at the bar, and orders a double martini on the rocks.

After he finishes the drink, he peeks inside his shirt pocket and orders another double martini. After he finishes that one, he again peeks inside his shirt pocket and orders a double martini.

The bartender says, 'Look, buddy, I'll bring ya martinis all night long. But you gotta tell me why you look inside your shirt pocket before you order a refill.'

The customer replies, 'I'm peeking at a photo of my wife. When she starts to look good, then I know it's time to go home.'

Joe walks into a bar. With him is a little guy a foot tall. Joe walks up to the bar and the little guy walks over to the piano and starts playing it and singing. The bartender, amazed at the sight of this little guy playing the piano and singing, moves over to Joe and talks to him.

'Hey,' he says, 'that little guy's really good. Where did you find him?'

Joe replies, 'I got him from my genie.'

'You've got a genie? Do you mind if I borrow him for a little while? I could really use some money.'

'No problem,' Joe says. 'Wish away.'

Whoosh! The genie appears.

'Wow,' gasps the bartender. 'I wish for ten thousand bucks!' With a bright flash and a crash of thunder there appears in the bar ten thousand ducks.

'Wait a minute,' cries the bartender. 'I asked for ten thousand bucks not ten thousand ducks!'

'Well,' says Joe, 'do you think I asked for a twelve-inch pianist?'

A man walks into a bar with a steak-and-kidney pie on his head. He walks over to the bartender and says, 'Can I have a beer please?'

The bartender gets him his beer but he can't stop staring at the pie on the man's head. Finally the bartender can't bite his tongue any longer.

'Excuse me Sir, but why do you have a steak-and-kidney pie on your head?'

The man replies, 'I always have a steak-and-kidney pie on my head on a Thursday.'

The bartender says, 'But it's Wednesday today.'

'Oh, I must look like a total moron then.'

A mangy looking guy goes into a bar and orders a drink. The bartender says, 'No way. I don't think you can pay for it.'

The guy says, 'You're right. I don't have any money, but if I show you something you haven't seen before, will you give me a drink?'

The bartender agrees.

So the guy and reaches into his coat pocket and pulls out a hamster. He puts the hamster on the bar and it runs to the end of the bar, down the bar, across the room and up onto the piano, jumps on the keyboard and starts playing Gershwin songs. The hamster is really good.

The bartender says, 'You're right. I've never seen anything like that before. That hamster is truly good on the piano.' The guy downs the drink and asks the bartender for another.

'Money or another miracle, or else no drink,' says the bartender. The guy reaches into his coat again and pulls out a frog. He puts the frog on the bar, and the frog starts to sing. He has a marvellous voice and great pitch – a fine singer. A stranger from the other end of the bar runs over to the guy and offers him $300 for the frog.

The guy says, 'It's a deal.'

He takes the $300 and gives the stranger the frog. The stranger runs out of the bar. The bartender says to the guy, 'Are you some kind of nut? You sold a singing frog for $300? It must have been worth millions. You must be crazy!'

'Not so,' says the guy. 'The hamster is also a ventriloquist.'

Warning: Consumption of alcohol may obstruct the space-time continuum. Small, and sometimes large, gaps of time may disappear from your memory bank.

A Scottish farmer walks into the neighbourhood pub, and orders a whisky.

'Ye see that fence over there?' he says to the bartender. 'Ah built it with me own two hands! Dug up the holes with me shovel, chopped doon the trees for the posts by me ownself, laid every last rail! But do they call me "McGregor the Fence-Builder?" No.'

He gulps down the whisky and orders another. 'Ye see that pier on the loch?' he continues, 'Ah built it me ownself, too. Swam oot into the loch to lay the foondations, laid doon every single board! But do they call me "McGregor the Pier-Builder"? No.' He takes another drink. 'But ye screw just one sheep...'

A young man sits down at the bar.

'What can I get you?' the bartender inquires.

'I want six shots of vodka,' says the young man.

'Six shots? Are you celebrating something?'

'Yeah, my first blowjob,' the young man answers.

'Well, in that case, let me give you a seventh on the house, son!'

'No offence, Sir. But if six shots won't get rid of the taste, nothing will.'

A mouse and a lion walk into a bar, and they're sitting there chugging away at a few ales when a giraffe walks in.

'Get a load of her,' says the mouse. 'I fancy that!'

'Well, why not try your luck?' says the lion.

So the mouse goes over to the giraffe and starts talking to her, and within five minutes they're out the door and gone into the night.

Next day, the lion is in the bar drinking away, and the mouse staggers in. He is absolutely stuffed.

The lion helps his pal up on to a stool, pours a drink down his throat and says, 'What the hell happened to you? I saw you leave with the giraffe, what happened after that? Was she all right?'

The mouse says, 'Yeah, she was really something else – we went out to dinner, had a couple of glasses of wine, and she invited me back to her place to spend the night. And oh, man! I've never had a night like it!'

'But how come you're so exhausted?' asks the lion.

'Well,' says the mouse, 'between the kissing and the screwing, I must have run a thousand miles.'

Three women, all with boyfriends named Leroy, are at a bar when one of the women says, 'I'm tired of getting my Leroy mixed up with your Leroy, and her Leroy mixed up with your Leroy. Why don't we all name our Leroys after a soft drink?'

The other two women agree, and the first woman says, 'OK then, let me go first. I name my Leroy 7-UP.'

The other two women ask her, 'Why 7-UP?'

'Because my Leroy has seven inches and it's always UP!'

All three women holler and hoot and slap each other on the back.

Then the second woman says, 'OK, I'm next, and I name my Leroy Mountain Dew.'

The other two women ask, 'Why Mountain Dew?'

'Because my Leroy can Mount and Dew me anytime.'

All three women holler and hoot and slap each other on the back.

The third woman then stands back and starts thinking and says, 'You know, those two Leroys were good, but I'm gonna name mine Jack Daniels.'

The other two women shout in unison, 'Jack Daniels? That's not a soft drink – that's a hard liquor!'

The third woman shouts, 'That's my Leroy!'

While a man at a bar savours a double martini, an attractive woman sits down next to him and orders a glass of orange juice.

The man turns to her and says, 'This is a special day. I'm celebrating.'

'I'm celebrating, too,' she replies, clinking glasses with him.

'What are you celebrating?' he asks.

'For years I've been trying to have a child,' she answers.

'Today my gynaecologist told me I'm pregnant!'

'Congratulations,' the man says, lifting his glass. 'As it happens, I'm a chicken farmer, and for years all my hens were infertile. But today they're finally fertile.'

'How did it happen?'

'I switched cocks.'

'What a coincidence,' she says, smiling.

BLONDES

A guy walks into a pub and sees a sign hanging over the bar that reads:

Cheese Sandwich: $1.50

Chicken Sandwich: $2.50

Hand Job: $10.00

He walks up to the bar and beckons to one of the three exceptionally attractive blondes serving drinks to an eager-looking group of men.

'Yes?' she inquires with a knowing smile. 'Can I help you?'

'I was wondering,' whispers the man, 'are you the one who gives the hand jobs?'

'Yes,' she purrs, 'indeed I am.'

The man replies, 'Well, wash your hands. I want a cheese sandwich!'

A blonde is morbidly obese, so her doctor puts her on a diet. 'Eat regularly for two days, then skip a day, and repeat this process for two weeks. The next time I see you, you'll have lost at least a few kilos.'

When the blonde returns, she's lost nearly eight kilos.

'That's incredible progress!' the doctor says. 'Did you follow my instructions?'

The blonde nods. 'I must admit, I thought I was going to drop dead that third day!'

'You mean from hunger?' asks the doctor.

'No, from all that skipping!'

While her husband is at work, a blonde decides that she is going to paint a couple of rooms in the house. The next day, straight after her husband leaves for work, she gets down to the task at hand. Her husband arrives home at 5.30 p.m. and smells the distinctive smell of paint. He walks into the living room and finds his wife lying on the floor in a pool of sweat.

He notices that she is wearing a ski jacket and a fur coat at the same time.

'Honey, are you OK?' he asks her.

'Yes,' she replies.

'Then what are you doing?' he asks.

'The directions on the paint say for best results, put on two coats.'

A highway patrolman pulls alongside a speeding car on the freeway. Glancing at the car, he is astounded to see that the blonde behind the wheel is knitting! Realising that she was oblivious to his flashing lights and siren, the cop cranks down his window, turns on his bullhorn and yells, 'Pull over!'

'No,' the blonde yells back. 'It's a scarf!'

A blonde arrives for her university final examination, which consists of questions requiring yes or no answers. She takes her seat in the examination hall and stares hopelessly at the exam paper for five minutes. Then in a fit of inspiration, she takes her purse out, removes a coin and starts tossing the coin and marking the answer sheet 'yes' for heads and 'no' for tails. Within half an hour she is finished, while the rest of the class is still writing madly. During the last few minutes, she is seen desperately throwing the coin, muttering and sweating. The moderator, alarmed, approaches her and asks what is going on.

'I finished the exam in half an hour,' she tells him, 'but I'm rechecking my answers.'

What's the mating call of a blonde?
    'I'm sooooo drunk!'

What do a bleach blonde and an aeroplane have in common?
    They both have black boxes.

Three seventeen-year-old girls – a blonde, a brunette and a redhead – are drinking in a bar. Suddenly, a cop walks in and the three run outside. He notices and follows them into an alley where there are three garbage bags but no sign of the girls. The police officer walks over to the first garbage bag and gives it a small kick.

The brunette, hiding inside, says, 'Meow.'

The officer says, 'Oh it's just some cats.'

He then kicks the next bag where the redhead is hiding.

She says, 'Woof, woof.'

The officer says, 'It's only some dogs.'

Finally, he kicks the last bag where the blonde is hiding.

She says, 'Potatoes, potatoes.'

A blonde, a redhead and a brunette are competing in the English Channel Breast Stroke Competition. The redhead wins and the brunette comes second. However, there is no sign of the final contestant. Hours and hours go by, causing grave concern and worry. Just as everyone is losing hope, the blonde finally arrives. The crowd is extremely happy and relieved to see her. They embrace the young woman as she comes ashore.

After all of the excitement dies down, the blonde leans over to the judge and whispers, 'I hate to be a bad loser, but I think those other girls used their arms.'

A blonde goes for a job interview in an office. The interviewer starts with the basics.

'So, can you tell us your age, please?'

The blonde counts carefully on her fingers for half a minute before replying, 'Uh…twenty-two!'

The interviewer tries another straightforward one to break the ice.

'And can you tell us your height, please?'

The young woman stands up and produces a measuring tape from her handbag. She then traps one end under her foot and extends the tape to the top of her head.

She checks the measurement and announces, 'A metre seventy!'

This isn't looking good so the interviewer goes for the real basics; something the interviewee won't have to count, measure, or look up.

'Just to confirm for our records, your name please?'

The blonde bobs her head from side to side for about ten seconds, mouthing something silently to herself, before replying, 'Mandy!'

The interviewer is completely baffled at this stage, and asks, 'What in the world were you doing when I asked you your name?'

'Oh, that!' replies the blonde. 'I was just running through that song, "Happy birthday to you, happy birthday to you, happy birthday dear…"'

THE DATING GAME

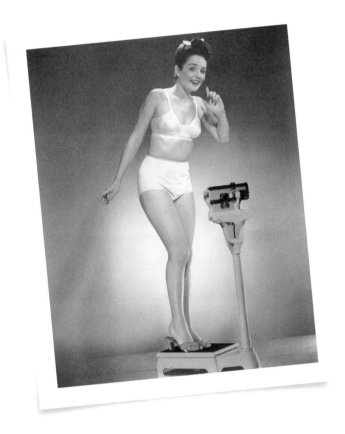

Alex takes his blind date to the carnival.

'What would you like to do first, Kate?' he asks.

'I want to get weighed,' she replies confidently.

They amble over to the weight guesser. The man looks at Kate and guesses 55 kg. Kate gets on the scale and it reads 53 kg, so she wins a prize.

Next the couple go on the Ferris wheel. When the ride is over, Alex again asks Kate what she would like to do.

'I want to get weighed,' she asserts.

So they go back to the weight guesser. Since they have been there before, the man guesses Kate's weight, and Alex loses his dollar. The couple walk around the carnival and again Alex asks what Kate would like to do next.

'I want to get weighed,' Kate responds firmly.

By this time, Alex thinks she is really strange and takes her home early, dropping in front of her house and driving off as fast as he can.

Kate's roommate, Laura, asks, 'How'd it go?'

Kate responds, 'Oh, Waura, it was wousy.'

A woman and a man are involved in a car accident; it's a bad one. Both of their cars are totally demolished but amazingly neither of them is hurt.

After they crawl out of their cars, the woman says, 'Wow, just look at our cars! There's nothing left, but fortunately we are unhurt. This must be a sign from God that we should meet and be friends and live together in peace for the rest of our days.'

The man replies, 'I agree with you completely. This must be a sign from God!'

The woman continues, 'And look at this, here's another miracle. My car is completely demolished but this bottle of wine didn't break. Surely God wants us to drink this wine and celebrate our good fortune.'

Then she hands the bottle to the man. The man nods his head in agreement, opens it, drinks half the bottle, and extends it back to the woman. Politely, the woman refuses to accept the bottle.

The man asks, 'Aren't you having any?'

The woman replies, 'No. I think I'll just wait for the police.'

A man is dating three women and wants to decide which to marry. He decides to give them a test. He gives each woman a present of $5000 and watches to see what they do with the money.

The first does a total makeover. She goes to a fancy beauty salon, gets her hair done, gets new make-up, and buys several new outfits to dress up very nicely for the man. She tells him that she has done this to be more attractive for him because she loves him. The man is impressed.

The second goes shopping to buy the man gifts. She gets him a new set of golf clubs, some new gizmos for his computer, and some expensive clothes. As she presents these gifts, she tells him that she has spent all the money on him because she loves him so much. Again, the man is impressed.

The third invests the money in the stock market. She earns several times the $5000. She gives him back his $5000 and reinvests the remainder in a joint account. She tells him that she wants to save for their future because she loves him. Obviously, the man is impressed.

He thinks for a long time about what each woman has done with the money he's given her. Then, he marries the one with the biggest breasts.

A couple was told to individually write a sentence using the words 'sex' and 'love'.

The woman wrote, 'When two people love each other very much, like Bob and I do, it is morally acceptable for them to engage in sex.'

Bob wrote, 'I love sex.'

PICK-UP LINES AND THEIR COMEBACKS

MAN: Haven't we met before?

WOMAN: Perhaps. I'm the receptionist at the Sexually Transmitted Disease clinic.

MAN: Is that seat empty?

WOMAN: Yes, and this one will be too if you sit down.

MAN: Your place or mine?

WOMAN: Both. You go to yours and I'll go to mine.

MAN: So what do you do for a living?

WOMAN: I'm a female impersonator.

MAN: Hey, baby, what's your sign?

WOMAN: Do not enter.

MAN: How do you like your eggs in the morning?

WOMAN: Unfertilised.

MAN: Hey, come on, we're both here at this bar for the same reason.

WOMAN: Yeah. Let's pick up some chicks.

MAN: I would go to the end of the world for you.

WOMAN: Yes, but would you stay there?

One night Paul takes his girlfriend Liza home.

They are about to kiss goodnight, but Paul is feeling a little horny, so he decides to push it further.

With an air of confidence, he leans with his hand against the wall. Smiling, he says to Liza, 'Sweetie, would you give me a blow job?'

Liza is shocked and embarrassed. 'Are you crazy? We're right outside my house!'

'Oh come on, honey! Who's going to see us at this hour?'

'No, please. Can you imagine what would happen if we got caught?'

'Oh come on, there's nobody around, they're all sleeping!' says Paul, becoming more horny as the conversation continues.

'No way. It's just too risky!'

'Oh please, please, I love you so much!'

'I love you too, but I just can't!'

'Yes you can. Please will you do it for me?'

'No, no. I just can't!'

'I'm begging you…'

'Oh, I just can't – '

Suddenly, the light on the stairs goes on, and Liza's sister shows up in her pyjamas.

'Look, dad says to go ahead and give the guy a blow job. Or if you don't want to, I can do it. Or mum can do it. Or if need be, Dad will come down himself and do it. But for God's sake, tell your stupid boyfriend to take his hand off the intercom.'

And God created Woman, and gave her three breasts. God spoke, saying to her, 'I have created thee as I see fit. Is there anything about thee that thou would prefer differently?'

And Woman spoke, saying, 'Lord, I am not made to birth whole litters. I need but two breasts.'

'Thou speakest wisely, as I have created thee with wisdom.'

There was a crack of lightning and a lingering odour of ozone, and it was done, and God stood holding the surplus breast in his hands.

'What are you going to do with that useless boob?' Woman asked.

And so it was, God created Man.

A boy and his date were parked on a back road some distance from town, doing what boys and girls do on back roads some distance from town. The girl stopped the boy.

'I really should have mentioned this earlier, but I'm actually a hooker and I charge $20 for sex,' she said.

The boy reluctantly paid her, and they did their thing.

After a cigarette, the boy just sat in the driver's seat looking out the window.

'Why aren't we going anywhere?' asked the girl.

'Well, I should have mentioned this before, but I'm actually a taxi driver, and the fare back to town is $25.'

My girlfriend suggested a book for me to read to enhance our relationship. It's called *Women are from Venus, Men are Wrong*.

TEN FACTS THAT EVERY MAN SHOULD KNOW ABOUT WOMEN

1 'Oh, nothing,' has an entirely different meaning in woman-language than it does in man-language.

2 Only women understand the reason for 'guest towels' and the 'good china'.

3 Women do not want an honest answer to the question, 'How do I look?'

4 PMS really stands for: Permissible Man-Slaughter, Preposterous Mood Swings or Punish My Spouse.

5 Men can never catch women checking out other men; but women will always catch men checking out other women.

6 Women love to talk on the phone. A woman can visit her girlfriend for two weeks, and upon returning home, she will call the same friend and they will talk for three hours.

7 Women can't use a map without turning the map to correspond to the direction that they are heading.

8 All women seek equality with men until it comes to sharing the closet, taking out the rubbish and picking up the bill.

9 Women never check to see if the seat of the toilet is down. They seem to prefer taking a flying butt leap towards the bowl, and then becoming enraged because 'you left the seat up' instead of taking two seconds and lowering it themselves.

10 Women don't really care about a sense of humour in a guy, despite claims to the contrary. You don't see women trampling over Brad Pitt to get to Danny DeVito, do you?

I t's a hot summer's night in 1957 and Johnny goes to pick up his date. At the front door, the girl's father invites him in.

'Lucy's not ready yet. Why don't you have a seat?' the father says. 'What are your plans for tonight?'

Johnny politely replies that they will probably go to dinner or a movie.

'Why don't the two of you go out and screw? I hear all the kids are doing it!'

Naturally, Johnny is taken aback, so he asks Lucy's dad to repeat himself.

'Yeah, Lucy really likes to screw; she'll screw all night if we let her!'

A few minutes later, Lucy comes downstairs in her poodle skirt. Johnny excitedly says goodbye to Lucy's father and escorts his date out the front door, full of anticipation.

Half an hour later, Lucy rushes back into the house, slamming the door behind her. Her eyes full of tears, she screams at her father, 'Dad, it's called the twist!'

Women want a relationship without the complication of unnecessary sex. Men want sex without the complication of an unnecessary relationship.

Dean saw an advertisement for a blow-up doll called Life-Like Tina which claimed she was 'so realistic you can't tell the difference!' As Dean had not had a girlfriend for a long time he ordered one, and waited in anticipation.

The supplier got the order from Dean, and the bloke who was mailing it couldn't believe how realistic 'Life-Like Tina' looked. When no one was around he decided to blow her up. He then thought that as she was inflated he might as well give her a bit of a test run. He had sex with the doll, meticulously washed it afterwards, packaged it up and posted it out to Dean.

A month later Dean rang the supplier.

'You know that Life-Like Tina blow up doll? I can't tell you how happy I am.'

'That's great!' said the supplier.

'It was a totally unbelievable experience,' enthused Dean.

'Realistic then?' asked the supplier.

'So realistic…I got syphilis.'

A young man is showing off his new sports car to his girlfriend. She is thrilled at the speed.

'If I do 250 kph, will you take off your clothes?' he smirks.

'OK,' says his adventurous girlfriend.

As he gets up to 250 kph, she peels off all her clothes.

Unable to keep his eyes on the road, the car skids on some gravel and flips over. The naked girl is thrown clear, but the boyfriend is jammed beneath the steering wheel.

'Go and get help!' he cries.

'But I can't! I'm naked and my clothes are gone!'

'Take my shoe,' he says, 'and cover yourself.'

Holding the shoe over her privates, the girl runs down the road and finds a service station. Still holding the shoe between her legs, she pleads to the service station proprietor for help.

'Please help me! My boyfriend's stuck!'

The proprietor looks at the shoe and says, 'There's nothing I can do. He's in too far.'

A guy stumbles from a bar with his keys in his hand.

A cop sees him and asks, 'Can I help you Sir?'

'Yesshh. Ssshhomebody shtole my carr.'

The cop asks him, 'Well, where did you last see it?'

The guy thinks for a while, 'At the end of dissh key.'

The cop looks at him and notices that his tool is hanging down from his pants.

'Sir, are you aware that you are exposing yourself to the whole world to see?'

The guy looks down woefully and says, 'Oh my goddd. Thheey got my girlfriend too!'

THIRTEEN PICK-UP LINES NEVER TO REPEAT

1 The word of the day is 'legs'. Let's go back to my place and spread the word.

2 That outfit would look great in a crumpled heap on my bedroom floor tomorrow morning.

3 I like every bone in your body, especially mine.

4 How about you sit on my lap and we'll see what pops up?

5 Is that a mirror in your pants, because I can see myself in them.

6 I want to kiss you passionately on the lips, and then move up to your belly-button.

7 Baby, I'd run a mile for your vertical smile.

8 I've got the F, the C and the K. All I need is U.

9 Hey baby, can I tickle your belly-button from the inside?

10 So do ya wanna see something really swell?

11 I may not be Fred Flintstone, but I sure can make your bed rock.

12 You have nice legs. What time do they open?

13 Hey that dress looks nice. Can I talk you out of it?

A virgin is going on her first date. Before she leaves the house, her grandmother sits her down.

'Let me tell you about young men, as they are all the same. First, he is going to try to kiss you. Don't let him do it. Then, he's going to try to feel your breasts. Don't let him do that either. Then he'll try to put his hand between your legs. Don't let him do it. But most importantly, he is going to try to get on top of you and have his way with you. Don't let him do that, it will disgrace the family.'

With her grandmother's advice, the girl goes on her date. The next day she can't wait to tell her grandmother about the date.

'It was exactly like you said!'

'Did you disgrace the family?' asks the grandmother anxiously.

'No way! When he tried, I turned over, got on top of him and disgraced his family!'

TEN THINGS THAT ONLY WOMEN UNDERSTAND

1 Cats' facial expressions.

2 The need for the same style of shoes in different colours.

3 Why bean sprouts aren't just weeds.

4 Fat clothes.

5 Taking a car trip without trying to beat your best time.

6 The difference between beige, off-white and eggshell.

7 Cutting your hair to make it grow faster.

8 Eyelash curlers.

9 The inaccuracy of every bathroom scale ever made.

10 That a cuddle does not necessarily need to turn into full-blown sex.

QUICK GIGGLES

Q How can you tell when a man is well hung?
A When you can just barely slip your finger in between his neck and the noose.

Q How do men exercise on the beach?
A By sucking in their stomachs every time they see a bikini.

Q How do you get a man to stop biting his nails?
A Make him wear shoes.

Q How do you keep your husband from reading your email?
A Rename the mail folder 'Instruction Manuals'.

Q What do most men consider a gourmet restaurant?
A Any place without a drive-through window.

Q What do you call the useless piece of skin on the end of a man's penis?
A His body.

Q What makes a man think about a candlelight dinner?
A A power failure.

Q What should you give a man who has everything?
A A woman to show him how to work it.

Q What do men and mascara have in common?
A They both run at the first sign of emotion.

Q What do you instantly know about a well-dressed man?
A His wife is good at picking out clothes.

Q What's a man's definition of a romantic evening?
A Sex.

Q What's a man's idea of honesty in a relationship?
A Telling you his real name.

Q Why can't men get mad cow disease?
A Because they're all pigs.

Q Why do men name their penises?
A Because they don't like the idea of having a stranger make 90% of their decisions.

Q Why do men whistle when they're sitting on the toilet?
A Because it helps them remember which end they need to wipe.

Q What do you call a woman who knows where her husband is every night?
A A widow.

Q When do you care for a man's company?
A When he owns it.

A husband and wife decide they need to use code to indicate that they want to have sex without letting their children in on it. They decide on the word 'typewriter'.

One day the husband tells his five-year-old daughter, 'Go tell your mummy that daddy needs to type a letter.'

The child tells her mother what her dad said, and her mum responds, 'Tell your daddy that he can't type a letter right now because there is a red ribbon in the typewriter.'

The child goes back to tell her father what mummy said.

A few days later the mum tells the daughter, 'Tell daddy that he can type that letter now.'

The child tells her father, returns to her mother and announces, 'Daddy said never mind about the typewriter, he already wrote the letter by hand.'

HOW MANY...DOES IT TAKE TO CHANGE A LIGHT BULB?

How many rich businessmen does it take to screw in a light bulb?
None. They screw in a hot tub.

How many psychiatrists does it take to change a light bulb?
Only one, but the light bulb has to want to change.

How many male chauvinist pigs does it take to change a light bulb?
None. Let the bitch cook in the dark.

How many men does it take to change a light bulb?
Four. One to actually change it, and three friends to brag to about how he screwed it.

How many women with PMS does it take to change a light bulb?
Six.

Why?
It just does OK!?

How many electrical engineers does it take to change a light bulb?
We don't know yet. They're still waiting on a part.

How many software developers does it take to change a light bulb?
The light bulb works fine on the system in my office.

How many perverts does it take to screw in a light bulb?
One, but it takes the entire staff of the emergency room to remove it.

How many actors does it take to change a light bulb?
One hundred. One to screw it in and the other ninety-nine to say 'I could've done that!'

How many Zen masters does it take to change a light bulb?
A tree in the golden forest.

How many Los Angeles policemen does it take to break a light bulb?
We did not break it. It fell down the stairs.

How many university lecturers does it take to change a light bulb?
Four. One to do it and three to co-author the paper.

How many university students does it take to change a light bulb?
Only one. But it takes nine years.

How many altos does it take to change a light bulb?
None. They can't get that high.

How many gods does it take to change a light bulb?
Two. One to hold the bulb and the other to rotate the planet.

How many cops does it take to change a light bulb?
None. It turned itself in.

How many authors does it take to change a light bulb?
Two. One to screw it almost in and the other to give it a surprising twist at the end.

How many sopranos does it take to change a light bulb?
One. She holds the bulb and the world revolves around her.

How many bass guitarists does it take to change a light bulb? Don't bother. Just leave it out. No-one will notice.

How many bass singers does it take to change a light bulb? None. They're so macho they prefer to walk in the dark and bang their shins.

Three blondes are attempting to change a light bulb. Finally, one of them decides to call 000.

'Help!' she says. 'We need help. We are three blondes changing a light bulb.'

'Hmm!' replies the operator. 'You put in a fresh bulb?'

'Yes.'

'The power in the house is on?'

'Of course.'

'And the switch is on?'

'Yes, yes.'

'And the bulb still won't light up?'

'No, it's working fine.'

'Then what's the problem?' asks the operator.

'We got dizzy spinning the ladder around and we all fell and hurt ourselves.'

THE SANCTITY OF MARRIAGE

A woman is at home when the doorbell rings.

When she opens the door, a man she has never seen asks her if she has a vagina. The woman slams the door in disbelief and embarrassment.

The same thing happens three days in a row. The woman decides to tell her husband.

The concerned husband has an idea.

'Tomorrow I won't go to work and when the man asks if you have a vagina say "yes". I will be hiding behind the door. We'll see what he has to say for himself then!'

The next day the man comes to the door again. When the woman opens the door he asks his standard question, 'Do you have a vagina?'

'Yes.'

The man then responds, 'Good! Then please tell your husband to stop screwing my wife!'

A husband and wife are divorcing and are in the process of arguing in front of a judge over custody of the children. The mother is asked to give her side of the story and explains that since she has brought the children into this world, she should retain custody of them. The judge nods his head in agreement, then turns to the man for his side of the story.

The man thinks for a few moments, then stands and says, 'Judge, when I put a quarter in a candy machine and a candy bar comes out, does it belong to me or the machine?'

Billy-Bob and Ray were talking one afternoon.

Billy-Bob tells Ray, 'Ya know, I reckon I'm 'bout ready for a holiday. Only this year I'm gonna do it a little different. The last few years, I took your advice about where to go. Three years ago you said to go to Hawaii. I went to Hawaii and Earline got pregnant. Then two years ago, you told me to go to the Bahamas, and Earline got pregnant again. Last year you suggested Tahiti and darned if Earline didn't get pregnant again.'

'So, what you gonna do this year that's different?' asks Ray.

'This year I'm taking Earline with me.'

A man in his 40s bought a new BMW and went out on the interstate for a nice evening drive. The top was down, the breeze was blowing through what was left of his hair, and he decided to open her up.

As the needle jumped up to 140 kph, he suddenly saw flashing red and blue lights behind him.

'There's no way they can catch a BMW,' he thought to himself and opened her up further.

The needle hit 150, 160…then the reality of the situation hit him.

'What the hell am I doing?' he thought and pulled over.

The cop came up to him, took his licence without a word, and examined it and the car. 'It's been a long day,' said the cop, 'this is the end of my shift, and it's Friday the 13th. I don't feel like more paperwork, so if you can give me an excuse for your driving that I haven't heard before, you can go.' The guy thinks for a second and says, 'Last week my wife ran off with a cop. I was afraid you were trying to give her back.'

'Have a nice weekend,' said the officer.

A little boy returning home from his first day at school said to his mother, 'Mum, what's sex?'.

His mother, who believed in all the most modern educational theories, gave him a detailed explanation, covering all aspects of the tricky subject.

When she had finished, the little lad produced an enrolment form which he had brought home from school and said, 'Yes, but how am I going to get all that into this one little square?'.

One morning, a man is relaxing and reading his paper. His wife comes up behind him and whacks him on the back of the head with a frying pan.

'What was that for?' asks the man, rubbing his head.

'Why is there a piece of paper in your pants pocket with the name Marybelle written on it?'

'Darling, don't you remember two weeks ago when I went to the horse races? Marybelle was the name of one of the horses I bet on!'

The wife apologises and pats him on his injured head.

Three days later the man is once again sitting in his chair reading and his wife cracks him on the back of the head once more.

'What's happened this time!?' he asks.

'Your horse rang.'

A new study has just been released mapping women's thoughts on marriage. The results were somewhat surprising: 85% of women think their ass has grown too big since getting married.

Another 10% of women think their ass is just as big as it was when they got married.

The other 5% say that they don't care, they love him and would have married him anyway.

A couple is in bed sleeping when there's a rat-a-tat-tat on the door. The husband rolls over and looks at the clock, it's 3.30 a.m.

'I'm not getting out of bed at this time,' he thinks, and rolls over.

There's a louder knock. So he drags himself out of bed, goes downstairs, opens the door, and a man is standing on the doorstep. It doesn't take the homeowner long to realise the man is drunk.

'Hi there,' slurs the stranger, 'Can you give me a push?'

'No, get lost. It's 3.30 a.m. and I was in bed.'

The man slams the door and goes back up to bed.

He tells his wife what happened and she says, 'That wasn't very nice of you. Remember that night we broke down in the pouring rain on the way to pick the kids up from the babysitter and you had to knock on that man's house to get us started again? What would have happened if he'd told us to get lost?'

'But the guy was drunk,' says the husband.

'It doesn't matter. He needs our help and it would be the Christian thing to help him.'

So the husband gets out of bed again, gets dressed and goes downstairs. He opens the door, and not being able to see the stranger anywhere, he shouts, 'Hey, do you still want a push?'

And he hears a voice cry out, 'Yes please.'

'Where are you?'

'Over here, on the swing.'

For sale by owner: Complete set of *Encyclopaedia Britannica*, 45 volumes. Excellent condition. $1000 or best offer. No longer needed. Got married last weekend. Wife knows f#*#ing everything.

There's no institution more worthy, more satisfying or more important than marriage – so my wife tells me!

A man spends six hours in a bar before rolling home to his wife blind drunk.

'Where have you been?' she demands.

'I've been to this amazing bar,' he slurs, rocking on his feet.

'It's called the Golden Saloon and everything there is golden. At the front there are two huge golden doors, the floors are golden and even the urinals are golden.'

'What rubbish,' snaps the wife. 'I don't believe a word of it.'

'Here,' said the husband, rummaging in his pocket for a piece of paper. 'Ring this number if you don't believe me.'

So the following day she phones the number on the slip of paper.

'Is this the Golden Saloon?' she asks.

'It is,' replies the bartender.

'Tell me,' says the wife, 'do you have two huge golden doors at the front of the building?'

'Sure do,' says the bartender.

'And do you have golden floors?'

'Yup.'

'What about golden urinals?'

There's a long pause and then the wife hears the bartender yell, 'Hey, Duke, I think I got a lead on the guy that pissed in your saxophone last night.'

A rich man and a poor man are Christmas shopping for their wives. The poor man asks the rich man what he is getting for his wife.

'I'm getting her a mink coat and a Porsche. I reckon if she doesn't like the mink coat, she'll like the Porsche. What about you?'

The poor man replies, 'I'm getting her a pair of slippers and a dildo. I reckon if she doesn't like the slippers she can go screw herself.'

A husband is watching TV when his wife comes in and interrupts, 'Darling, could you fix the light in the hallway? It's been flickering for weeks.'

He shouts angrily, 'Fix the light. Do I have General Electric written on my forehead? I don't think so.'

'Well then, could you fix the fridge door? It won't close properly.'

'Fix the fridge door. Do I have Westinghouse written on my forehead? I don't think so.'

'Fine,' she says. 'Then could you at least fix the steps on the porch? They're about to break.'

'Fix the steps. Do I have Home Hardware written on my forehead? I don't think so. I've had enough of you. I'm going to the bar!'

He slams the door and goes to the bar. After a while, he starts to feel guilty about how he treated his wife, and decides to go home. As he walks up the steps to the porch, he notices they are already fixed. Upon entering the house, he sees the hall light is working. Walking through the kitchen, he notices the fridge door is fixed.

'Sweetheart, how did you get all this fixed?'

'Well, when you left, I sat outside and wept. A nice young man asked me what had happened and I told him. He offered to do all the repairs, and all I had to do was either screw him or bake him a cake.'

The husband asks, 'So, what kind of cake did you bake him?'

'Bake a cake? Do I have Sara Lee written on my forehead? I don't think so.'

A woman goes into a store to buy her husband a pet for his birthday. After looking around, she finds that all the pets are very expensive. She tells the clerk she wants to buy a pet, but she doesn't want to spend a fortune.

'Well,' says the clerk. 'I have a very large bullfrog. They say it's been trained to give blowjobs.'

'Blowjobs!'

'It hasn't been proven, but we've sold thirty of them this month,' he says.

The woman thinks it will make a great gag gift, and what if it's true…no more blowjobs for her. So she buys the frog and gives it to her husband. When she explains froggy's ability to him, he is extremely sceptical and laughs it off.

The woman goes to bed happy, thinking she may never need to perform this less than riveting act again. In the middle of the night, she is awakened by the noise of pots and pans flying everywhere. She runs downstairs to the kitchen, only to find her husband and the frog reading cookbooks.

'What are you two doing at this hour?' she asks.

The husband replies, 'If I can teach this frog to cook, you're out of here.'

A young couple, just married, are in the honeymoon suite on their wedding night. As they undress for bed, the husband, who is a big burly man, tosses his pants to his bride and says, 'Here put these on.'

She puts them on and the waist is twice the size of her body.

'I can't wear your pants,' she says.

'That's right,' says the husband, 'and don't you forget it. I'm the one who wears the pants in this family!'

With that she flips him her panties and says, 'Try these on.'

He tries them on and finds he can only get them on as far as his kneecap.

He says, 'I can't get into your panties.'

She says, 'That's right, and that's the way it's going to be until your attitude changes.'

Did you hear about the new edition of *Playboy* for married men?

It has the same centrefold every month.

A man and a woman are having dinner in a fine restaurant. Their waitress, taking another order at a table a few paces away, notices that the man is slowly sliding down his chair and under the table, with the woman acting unconcerned. The waitress watches as the man slides all the way down his chair and out of sight under the table. Still, the woman dining across from him appears calm and unruffled, apparently unaware that her dining companion has disappeared.

After the waitress finishes taking the order, she comes over to the table and says to the woman, 'Pardon me, Ma'am, but I think your husband just slid under the table.'

The woman calmly looks up at her and replies firmly, 'No he didn't. He just walked in the door.'

A woman bursts through the front door of her house. She finds her husband and yells, 'Pack your bags honey, I just won the lottery! Ten million bucks!'

'That's incredible darling!' he replies, 'Should I pack for the beach or for the mountains?'

'I don't care! Just piss off!'

A man and a woman are married. One day the husband, thinking he's being funny, grabs his wife's boobs as she's getting into the shower and says to her, 'You know, if these were firm, you wouldn't need a bra!'

His wife is really angry; it was a rude thing to say. The next day, as she's getting out of the shower, he grabs her arse and says, 'You know, if this was firm, you wouldn't need a girdle!'

Now the wife is really pissed off and she's plotting her revenge. So the next day, as her husband is getting out of the shower, she grabs his dick and says, 'You know, if this was firm I wouldn't need your brother!'

A newly married couple move into a house and the wife notices a mirror hanging on the wall.

She goes up to it and says, 'Mirror Mirror on the wall, what part of my body does my husband like most of all?'

And the mirror replies, 'Your tits.'

She then says, 'Mirror Mirror on the wall, give me size double D.'

And hey presto, she gets really big tits. Excitedly she rushes downstairs to show her husband, who is amazed upon seeing her.

He asks her what happened and she tells him about the mirror.

The husband rushes upstairs to the mirror and says, 'Mirror Mirror on the wall, what part of my body does my wife like most of all?'

'Your dick.'

'Mirror Mirror on the wall, make my dick touch the floor.'

So his legs fall off.

A businessman is on an overnight train trip with his secretary.

They both retire to their respective rooms but a while later the secretary comes into the man's room and says, 'Excuse me Mr Johnston, but could you please pass me a blanket?'

Mr Johnston asks, 'Do you want to be Mrs Johnston for the night?'

The secretary thinks for a moment then says, 'That would be nice.'

To this Mr Johnston says, 'Good. Get your own bloody blanket.'

A man has six children and is very proud of his achievement. He is so proud of himself that he starts calling his wife Mother of Six, in spite of her objections.

One night they go to a party. The man decides that it's time to go home, and wants to find out if his wife is ready to leave as well. He shouts at the top of his voice, 'Shall we go home Mother of Six?'

His wife, irritated by her husband's lack of discretion, shouts back, 'Anytime you're ready, Father of Four!'

A man is drunk and in no shape to drive, so he wisely leaves his car parked and walks home. As he is walking unsteadily along, he is stopped by a policeman.

'What are you doing out here at 2 a.m.?' asks the officer.

'I'm going to a lecture,' the man says.

'And who is going to give a lecture at this hour?' the cop asks.

'My wife,' says the man.

10 THINGS NOT TO SAY TO YOUR PREGNANT WIFE

1 'Not to imply anything, but I don't think the kid weighs 10 kg.'

2 'Y'know, looking at her, you'd never guess that Angelina Jolie had twins.'

3 'Well, couldn't they induce labour? The 25th is the grand final.'

4 'Fred at the office passed a stone the size of a pea. Boy, that's gotta hurt.'

5 'I'm jealous. Why can't men experience the joy of childbirth?'

6 'Are your ankles supposed to look like that?'

7 'Get your own ice cream.'

8 'Geez, you're looking awfully puffy today.'

9 'Got milk?'

10 'Man! That rose tattoo on your hip is the size of Madagascar!'

When a woman says, 'C'mon, this place is a mess! You and I need to clean. Your pants are on the floor and you'll have no clothes if we don't do laundry now!'

A man hears, 'C'mon…blah, blah, blah…You and I…blah, blah, blah, blah, blah…on the floor…blah, blah, blah…no clothes…blah, blah, blah, blah…now!'

A husband and wife who have been married twenty years were doing some work in the back yard. The man was working hard cleaning the barbecue grill while his wife was bending over the flower bed, weeding.

The man says to his wife, 'Your bottom is almost as wide as this grill!'

The wife ignores the remark and continues weeding.

A few minutes later, the husband takes his measuring tape and measures the grill, then he goes over to his wife, measures her backside and proclaims, 'Wow, your bottom really *is* as wide as the grill!'

She ignores this remark as well.

That night in bed, the husband starts to feel horny. The wife calmly responds, 'If you think I'm going to fire up the grill for one little sausage, you are sadly mistaken.'

Harold's wife bought a new line of expensive cosmetics guaranteed to make her look years younger.

After applying her 'miracle' products, she asked, 'Darling, honestly, what age would you say I am?'

Looking over her carefully, Harold replied, 'Judging from your skin, 20; your hair, 18; and your figure, 25.'

'Oh, you flatter me!'

'Hey, wait a minute! I haven't added them up yet.'

A husband is sent out by his wife to buy some fruit and vegetables. But they have to be organic. He goes to the market and has a good look around but can't find any.

So he grabs an old, tired-looking employee and says, 'These vegetables are for my wife. Have they been sprayed with any poisonous chemicals?'

The produce guy looks at him and says, 'No. You'll have to do that yourself.'

A man goes to the police station wanting to speak to the burglar who broke into his house the night before.

'You'll get your chance in court,' says the desk sergeant.

'No, no, no!' says the man. 'I want to know how he got into the house without waking my wife. I've been trying to do that for years!'

How many men does it take to open a beer?
None. It should be opened by the time she brings it.

Why do women have smaller feet then men?
So they can stand closer to the kitchen sink.

How do you fix a woman's watch?
You don't. There's a clock on the oven.

Why do men pass more gas than women do?
Because women don't shut up long enough to build up pressure.

DATING VS MARRIAGE

When you are dating…He takes you out to have a good time.
When you are married…He brings home a six pack and says, 'What are you going to drink?'
When you are dating…You are turned on at the sight of him naked.
When you are married…You think to yourself, 'Was he always this hairy?'
When you are dating…You enjoy foreplay.
When you are married…You tell him, 'If we have sex, will you leave me alone?'
When you are dating…You picture the two of you together, growing old together.
When you are married…You wonder who will die first.
When you are dating…He understands if you aren't in the mood.
When you are married…He says, 'It's your job.'
When you are dating…He understands that you have male friends.
When you are married…He thinks they are all out to steal you away.
When you are dating…He likes to discuss things.
When you are married…He develops a blank stare.
When you are dating…He calls you by name.
When you are married…He calls you 'Hey' and refers to you when speaking to others as 'She'.

Three married couples aged in their 20s, 30s and 40s wish to join the Orthodox Church of Sexual Repression. Near the end of the interview, the priest informs them that before they can be accepted they will have to pass one small test. They will have to abstain from all sex for a month. They agree to try.

A month later, they are having their final interview with the cleric. He asks the couple in their 40s how they went.

'Well, it wasn't too hard. I spent a lot of time in the workshop and my partner has a garden, so we had plenty of other things to do. We did OK,' the husband says.

'Very good, my children,' says the priest. 'You are welcome in the Church.'

'And how well did you manage?' he asks the couple in their 30s.

'It was pretty difficult,' the husband answers. 'We thought about it all the time. We had to sleep in different beds and we prayed a lot. But we were celibate for the entire month.'

'Very good, my children, you also are welcome in the Church. And how about you?' he asks the couple in their 20s.

'Not too good, I'm afraid, Father. We did OK for the first week,' the man says sheepishly. 'By the second week we were going crazy with lust. Then one day during the third week my wife dropped a head of lettuce, and when she bent over to pick it up, I weakened and took her right there.'

'I'm sorry my son, but you are not welcome in the Church.'

'Yeah, and we're not too welcome in the supermarket anymore, either.'

HE SAYS; SHE SAYS

HE SAYS: I don't know why you wear a bra; you've got nothing to put in it.

SHE SAYS: You wear briefs, don't you?

HE SAYS: Do you love me just because my father left me a fortune?

SHE SAYS: Not at all honey, I would love you no matter who left you the money.

HE SAYS: This coffee isn't fit for a pig!

SHE SAYS: No problem, I'll get you some that is.

SHE SAYS: What do you mean by coming home half drunk?

HE SAYS: It's not my fault. I ran out of money.

HE SAYS: Since I first laid eyes on you, I've wanted to make love to you in the worst way.

SHE SAYS: Well, you succeeded.

HE SAYS: Why do you women always try to impress us with your looks, not with your brains?

SHE SAYS: Because there is a bigger chance that a man is a moron than he is blind.

HE SAYS: What have you been doing with all the grocery money I gave you?

SHE SAYS: Turn sideways and look in the mirror.

HE SAYS: Let's go out and have some fun tonight.

SHE SAYS: OK, but if you get home before I do, leave the hall light on.

DEFINITIONS BY GENDER

Butt (but) n.

FEMALE: The part of the body that every item of clothing manufactured makes look bigger.

MALE: What you slap when someone's scored a goal. Also useful for mooning.

Commitment (ko-mit-ment) n.

FEMALE: A desire to get married and raise a family.

MALE: Not trying to pick up other women while out with one's girlfriend.

Communication (ko-myoo-ni-kay-shon) n.

FEMALE: The open sharing of thoughts and feelings with one's partner.

MALE: Scratching out a note before suddenly taking off for a weekend with the boys.

Entertainment (en-ter-tayn-ment) n.

FEMALE: A good movie, concert, play or book.

MALE: Anything that can be done while drinking.

Flatulence (flach-u-lens) n.

FEMALE: An embarrassing by-product of digestion.

MALE: An endless source of entertainment, self-expression and male bonding.

Making love (may-king luv) n.

    FEMALE: The greatest expression of intimacy a couple can achieve.

    MALE: Call it whatever you want just as long as we end up in bed.

Thingy (thing-ee) n.

    FEMALE: Any part under a car's hood.

    MALE: The strap fastener on a woman's bra.

Vulnerable (vul-ne-ra-bel) adj.

    FEMALE: Fully opening up emotionally to another.

    MALE: Riding a motorbike without a helmet.

A husband has just finished reading the book *Man of the House*. He marches up to his wife. Pointing a finger in her face, he says, 'From now on, I want you to know that I am the man of this house, and my word is law! Now this is what

I want you to do. I want you to prepare me a delicious meal, and when I've finished eating it, I expect a delectable dessert. Then, I want you to run me a bath, so I can unwind. And when I'm finished with the bath, guess who's going to dress me and comb my hair?'

His wife replied, 'The funeral director would be my guess.'

THE BENEFITS OF BEING A WOMAN

- Our boyfriends' clothes make us look elfin and gorgeous. Guys look like complete idiots in ours.
- We can be groupies. Male groupies are stalkers.
- We can cry and get off speeding fines.
- Men die earlier, so we get to cash in on the life insurance.
- We don't look like a frog in a blender when dancing.
- Free drinks, free dinners.
- We can hug our friends without wondering if they're gay.
- We can hug our friends without wondering if we're gay.
- It's possible to live our whole lives without ever taking a group shower.
- We don't have to fart to amuse ourselves.
- If we forget to shave, no-one has to know.
- We can congratulate our team-mate without ever touching her bum.
- If we have a zit, we know how to conceal it.
- We don't have to reach down every so often to make sure our privates are still there.
- If we're dumb, some people will find it cute.
- We don't have to memorise *Jackass* or *The Simpsons* to fit in.
- If we marry someone twenty years younger, we're aware that we look like an idiot.

- We know that there are times when chocolate really can solve all your problems.
- We can fully assess a person just by looking at their shoes.

BENEFITS OF BEING A MAN

- Your ass is never a factor in a job interview.
- Your orgasms are real. Always.
- Your last name stays put.
- Wedding plans take care of themselves.
- You don't have to curl up next to a hairy bottom every night.
- Chocolate is just another snack.
- Foreplay is optional.
- Car mechanics tell you the truth.
- You don't give a rat's ass if someone notices your new haircut.
- The world is your urinal.
- Hot wax never comes near your pubic area.
- Same work…more pay.
- Wrinkles add character.
- You don't have to leave the room to make emergency crotch adjustments.
- Wedding dress $2000; Tux rental $100. Nuff said.
- People never glance at your chest when you're talking to them.
- Princess Di's death was just another obituary.
- New shoes don't cut, blister or irreparably damage your feet.

- Porn movies are designed with you in mind.
- Your pals can be trusted never to trap you with, 'So, notice anything different?'

A man walks into a store to buy a Barbie doll for his daughter.

'How much is that Barbie in the window?' he asks the shop assistant.

In a condescending manner she responds, 'Which Barbie? We have Barbie Goes to the Gym for $19.95, Barbie Goes to the Ball for $19.95, Barbie Goes Shopping for $19.95, Barbie Goes to the Beach for $19.95, Barbie Goes Nightclubbing for $19.95 and Divorced Barbie for $265.'

The guy asks, 'Why is Divorced Barbie $265 when all the others are only $19.95?'

'That's obvious,' the assistant states, 'Divorced Barbie comes with Ken's house, Ken's car, Ken's boat and Ken's furniture.'

Two women are having lunch together, discussing the merits of cosmetic surgery.

The first woman says, 'I need to be honest with you, I'm getting a boob job.'

The second woman says, 'Oh that's nothing, I'm thinking of having my arsehole bleached.'

The first replies, 'Funny, I just can't picture your husband as a blonde.'

A guy was talking to his friend, 'I don't know what to get my wife for her birthday. She has everything, and besides, she can afford to buy anything she wants. What should I do?'

His friend replied, 'I have an idea. Why don't you make up a certificate that says she can have two hours of great sex, any way she wants it. She'll probably be thrilled!'

The first guy went away and wrote out a certificate.

The next day his friend asks, 'How did it turn out?'

'Well, she loved it. She thanked me, hugged and kissed me, and ran out the door yelling, "I'll see you in two hours"…'

POLITICS

The CIA were conducting a job interview for only highly qualified people. After all the background checks, interviews and testing were done, there were three finalists: two men and a woman.

For the final test, the CIA agents took one of the men to a large metal door and handed him a gun.

'We must know that you will follow your instructions, no matter what the circumstances,' said the agent.

'Inside this room, you will find your wife sitting in a chair. Kill her!'

The man said, 'You can't be serious. I could never shoot my wife.'

'Then you're not the right man for this job. Take your wife and go home.'

The second man was given the same instructions. He took the gun and went into the room. All was quiet for about five minutes.

Then the man came out with tears in his eyes. 'I tried, but I can't kill my wife.'

'You don't have what it takes. Take your wife and go home.'

Finally, it was the woman's turn. She was given the same instructions to kill her husband. She took the gun and went into the room. Shots were heard, one shot after another.

They heard screaming, crashing, banging on the walls.

After a few minutes, all was quiet. The door opened slowly and there stood the woman. She wiped the sweat from her brow.

'This gun is loaded with blanks,' she said. 'I had to beat him to death with the chair.'

The president was out walking on a beautiful snowy day, when he saw that somebody had urinated on the White House lawn. In large loopy letters it spelt out 'the president sucks'.

Infuriated, he called on the secret service to work out who had done it. In a few hours, they came to him and told him that there was some bad news and some worse news.

'Give me the bad news first,' said the president.

'The bad news is that the urine is the vice president's.'

'How could he do this to me? What could be worse than that?'

'The handwriting is the first lady's.'

A son asked his father, 'What can you tell me about politics? I have to learn about it for school tomorrow.'

The father thought a little and said, 'OK, son, the best way I can describe politics is to use an analogy. Let's say that I'm a capitalist because I'm the breadwinner. Your mother will be the government because she controls everything. Our maid will be the working class because she works for us. You will be the people because you answer to us. And your baby brother will be the future. Does that help any?'

The little boy said, 'Well, dad, I don't know, but I'll think about what you said.'

Later that night, after everyone had gone to bed, the little boy was awoken by his baby brother's crying. He went to his brother and realised that he had a dirty nappy. So he went down the hall to his parent's bedroom to tell his parents.

His father's side of the bed was empty, and try as he could his mother wouldn't wake up. He then saw a light on in the guest room down the hall, and through the crack in the door he saw that his father was in bed with the maid.

The son then turned and went back to bed. The next morning, he said to his father at the breakfast table, 'Dad, I think I understand politics much better now.'

'Excellent, my boy,' he answered, 'What have you learned?'

The little boy thought for a minute and said, 'I learned that capitalism is screwing the working class, government is sound asleep ignoring the people, and the future's full of crap.'

LET'S GET IT ON

Husband: 'Why don't you scream my name when you orgasm?'

Wife: 'Because you're never there.'

A man, a dog and a sheep are stranded on an island with no food or water, nothing. Months have passed and there is no hope of them ever getting off this island; they are pretty much going to die there. One night, as they all go to sleep, the man quietly gets up and moves close to the sheep and puts his arm round it. He then carefully flips the sheep onto its stomach, pulls his pants down, and flops his dick out.

Suddenly, the dog gets up and starts barking at the man and scares him away from the sheep. The days and nights pass and the more the man tries to have sex with the sheep, the more the dog scares him off.

One morning they all go for a walk along the beach looking for ships and boats. Suddenly, the man hears screaming coming from the sea. He looks over at the water and sees a woman drowning a few metres from shore, so he rushes down, dives in and saves the helpless women, and brings her back to the beach. The man looks at the woman and realises that she is very, very hot. She has big boobs, a hot arse and sexy legs.

The woman says to the man, 'You saved my life, anything you want I'll do, anything.'

The man thinks for a while and finally says, 'You couldn't take the dog for a walk, could you?'

'So let me get this straight,' the prosecutor says to the defendant, 'you came home from work early and found your wife in bed with a strange man.'

'That's correct,' says the defendant.

'You then take out a pistol and shoot your wife, killing her.'

'That's correct.'

'Then my question to you is, why did you shoot your wife and not her lover?' asked the prosecutor.

'It seemed easier than shooting a different man every day.'

One day Mrs Jones went to have a talk with the minister at the local church.

'Reverend,' she said, 'I have a problem, my husband keeps falling asleep during your sermons. It's very embarrassing. What should I do?'

'I have an idea,' said the minister. 'Take this hat-pin with you. I will be able to tell when Mr Jones is sleeping, and I will motion to you at specific times. When I motion, you give him a good poke in the leg.'

In church the following Sunday, Mr Jones dozed off. Noticing this, the preacher put his plan to work.

'And who made the ultimate sacrifice for you?' he said, nodding to Mrs Jones.

'Jesus!' Jones cried, as his wife jabbed him in the leg with the hat-pin.

'Yes, you are right, Mr Jones,' said the minister.

Soon, Mr Jones nodded off again. Again, the minister noticed.

'Who is your redeemer?' he asked the congregation, motioning towards Mrs Jones.

'Oh God!' Mr Jones cried out, as he was stuck again with the hat-pin.

'Right again,' said the minister, smiling.

Before long, Mr Jones again winked off. However, this time the minister did not notice. As he picked up the tempo of his sermon, he made a motion that Mrs Jones mistook as the signal to bayonet her husband with the hat-pin again.

The minister asked, 'And what did Eve say to Adam after she bore him his 99th son?'

Mrs Jones poked her husband, who yelled, 'You stick that goddamned thing in me one more time and I'll break it in half and shove it up your arse!'

Jeff and Mike are killed in an accident and as Jeff arrives at the pearly gates, he is met by St Peter.

'Where's my friend Mike?' Jeff asks the old saint.

St Peter replies, 'Mike wasn't as fortunate as you, instead of heaven, he went in the other direction.'

Jeff is deeply concerned by this and asks, 'Well, could I see Mike just one more time?'

St Peter agrees to this, so they walk over to the edge of heaven and look down. Jeff sees Mike down in hell with a sexy blonde on one side of him and a keg of beer on the other.

'I really don't mean to complain,' Jeff says, 'but Mike seems to be having a pretty nice time down in hell.'

'Look a little closer,' says St Peter. 'The keg has a hole in it, and the blonde doesn't.'

WHY CHOCOLATE IS BETTER THAN SEX

1 Chocolate satisfies even when it has gone soft.

2 You can have chocolate in front of your mother.

3 If you bite the nuts too hard the chocolate won't mind.

4 The word 'commitment' doesn't scare off chocolate.

5 You can have chocolate on top of your workbench or desk during working hours without upsetting your co-workers.

6 You don't get hairs in your mouth with chocolate.

7 With chocolate there's no need to fake it.

8 Chocolate doesn't make you pregnant.

9 When you have chocolate it does not keep your neighbours awake.

10 With chocolate, size doesn't matter.

HOW TO SATISFY A WOMAN EVERY TIME

Caress, praise, pamper, relish, savour, massage, make plans, fix, empathise, serenade, compliment, support, feed, tantalise, bathe, humour, placate, stimulate, stroke, console, purr, hug, coddle, excite, pacify, protect, phone, correspond, anticipate, nuzzle, smooch, toast, minister to, forgive, sacrifice for, ply, accessorise, leave, return, beseech, sublimate, entertain, charm, lug, drag, crawl, treat equally, spackle, oblige, fascinate, attend, implore, bawl, shower, shave, trust, grovel, ignore, defend, coax, clothe, brag about, acquiesce, fuse, fizz, rationalise, detoxify, sanctify, help, acknowledge, polish, upgrade, spoil, embrace, accept, butter-up, hear, understand, jitterbug, locomote, beg, plead, borrow, steal, climb, swim, nurse, resuscitate, repair, patch, super-glue, respect, entertain, calm, allay, kill for, die for, dream of, promise, deliver, tease, flirt, commit, enlist, pine, cajole, murmur, snuggle, snoozle, snurfle, elevate, enervate, alleviate, spot-weld, serve, rub, rib, salve, bite, taste, nibble, gratify, take her places, scuttle like a crab on the ocean floor of her existence, diddle, doodle, hokey-pokey, hanky-panky, crystal blue, persuade, flip, flop, fly, don't care if I die, swing, slip, slide, slather, mollycoddle, squeeze, moisturise, humidify, lather, tingle, slam-dunk, keep on rockin' in the free world, wet, slicken, undulate, gelatinise, brush, tingle, dribble, drip, dry, knead, fluff, fold, ingratiate, indulge, wow, dazzle, amaze, flabbergast, enchant, idolise and worship, and then go back, Jack, and do it again.

HOW TO SATISFY A MAN EVERY TIME

Show up naked…with beer.

A woman is feeling a bit down in the dumps and decides to treat herself to a meal at a very expensive restaurant. She manages to get a table, even though the place is very busy, and she enjoys a delicious meal on her own. Aware of her financial limitations, she doesn't go overboard but does make sure she enjoys herself. When the head waiter brings the bill, she's horrified to see the total – $250! She didn't expect this at all. Realising there's no point complaining, she hands over her credit card.

When the waiter returns with the slip for her to sign, she asks him, 'Would you mind holding my breasts while I sign my name please?'

The waiter is taken aback. In all his years in the job he's never been asked that before. But he is always eager to please the customer and he obliges. When the woman gets up to leave, the waiter's curiosity gets the better of him. He catches up with her at the door.

'I'm sorry to bother you Miss but I'd like to know why you asked me to do that just now.'

'Oh it's quite simple really,' she replies, 'I love to have my breasts held when I'm being screwed!'

A passenger plane runs into a terrible storm. The plane gets pounded by rain, hail, wind and lightning. The passengers are screaming. They are sure the plane is going to crash and they are all going to die.

At the height of the storm, a young woman jumps up and exclaims, 'I can't take this anymore! I can't just sit here and die like an animal, strapped into a chair. If I am going to die, let me die feeling like a woman. Is there anyone here man enough to make me feel like a woman?'

She sees a raised hand in the back and a muscular man starts to walk up to her seat. As he approaches her, he takes off his shirt. She can see the man's muscles even in the poor lighting of the plane.

He stands in front of her, shirt in hand and says to her, 'I can make you feel like a woman before you die. Are you interested?'

She nods her head yes.

The man hands her his shirt and says, 'Here. Iron this.'

A husband walks into the bedroom holding two headache tablets and a glass of water.

'What's that for?' his wife asks.

'It's for your headache.'

'But I don't have a headache.'

'Gotcha!'

A very shy guy goes into a bar and sees a beautiful woman sitting at the bar.

After an hour of gathering up his courage, he finally goes over to her and asks, tentatively, 'Um, would you mind if I chatted with you for a while?'

She responds by yelling, at the top of her lungs, 'No! I won't sleep with you tonight!'

Everyone in the bar is now staring at them. Naturally, the guy is hopelessly and completely embarrassed and he slinks back to his table.

After a few minutes, the woman walks over to him and apologises.

She smiles at him and says, 'I'm sorry if I embarrassed you. You see, I'm a graduate student in psychology, and I'm studying how people respond to embarrassing situations.'

To which he responds, at the top of his lungs, 'What do you mean $200?'

A man and his wife have been stranded on a deserted island for many years. One day another man washes up on shore. The new man and the wife are very attracted to each other right away, but realise certain protocols must be observed.

The husband, however, is very glad to see the second man.

'Now we will be able to have three people doing eight-hour shifts in the watchtower, rather than two people doing twelve-hour shifts.'

The new man is only too happy to help and volunteers to do the first shift. He climbs up the tower and is soon standing watch. Soon the husband and wife start placing stones in a circle to make a fire to cook supper. The second man yells down, 'Hey, no screwing!'

They yell back, 'We're not screwing!'

A few minutes later they start to put driftwood into the stone circle. Again the second man yells down, 'Hey, no screwing!'

Again they yell back, 'We're not screwing!'

Later they are putting palm leaves on the roof of their shack to patch leaks. Once again the second man yells down, 'Hey, I said no screwing!'

They yell back, 'We're not screwing!'

Finally the shift is over so the second man climbs down from the tower and the husband starts to climb up. He's not even halfway up before the wife and the second man are screwing each other's brains out.

The husband looks out from the tower and says, 'Son-of-a-gun. From up here it does look like they're screwing.'

A man is required to report to the taxation department. He asks his accountant for advice on what to wear.

'Wear your shabbiest clothing. Let them think you are a pauper,' says the accountant.

Then he asks his lawyer the same question, but gets the opposite advice.

'Do not let them intimidate you. Wear your most elegant suit and tie,' says his lawyer.

Confused, the man goes to his priest, tells him of the conflicting advice, and requests some resolution of the dilemma.

'Let me tell you a story,' replies the priest. 'A woman, about to be married, asks her mother what to wear on her wedding night. "Wear a heavy, long, flannel nightgown that goes right up to your neck," she says.

'But when she asks her best friend, she gets conflicting advice. "Wear your most sexy negligee, with a V neck right down to your navel," the friend says.'

The man protests, 'What does all this have to do with my problem with the taxation department?'

'No matter what you wear,' replies the priest. 'You're going to get screwed.'

THE FIVE SECRETS TO A GREAT RELATIONSHIP (FEMALE VERSION)

1 It is important to find a man who works around the house, occasionally cooks and cleans and who has a job.

2 It is important to find a man who makes you laugh.

3 It is important to find a man who is dependable, respectful and doesn't lie.

4 It is important to find a man who's good in bed and who loves to have sex with you.

5 It is important that these four men never meet.

Time after time, night after night Tom just can't last long while having sex with his wife. He feels horrible, he feels like he is disappointing her.

She constantly reassures him saying, 'Honey, don't worry about it. It's alright.'

Finally, he decides to see a doctor.

The doctor looks at him and says, 'Believe it or not, it's not an uncommon problem. Have you ever tried masturbating before you have sex with your wife?'

Tom replies, 'No.'

'Well,' the doctor continues, 'if you do, it will take you longer to come when you're having sex with your wife.'

Tom smiles and says, 'Thanks doc, I'll give it a try.'

The next day while Tom is at work, he receives a call from his wife. She warns him that she is extremely horny and that she is going to attack him the moment he walks through the door. This gets him excited, but then he realises that if she attacks him when he walks through the door, he won't be able to try out the doctor's suggestion. Tom tries to think of somewhere he can go to try his new technique. He can't do it at his desk. The mail room is too risky. So is the toilet. He decides he will just pull over on his way home, get under his car and act like he's working on it, nobody will know.

On his way home he finds a nice open spot on the side of the road and pulls over. He gets under the car, closes his eyes, and proceeds to 'check the axle' under his car. About five minutes later he feels a tug on his pants, and not wanting to see who it is, he asks, 'Who is it?'

'It's the police. What do you think you're doing?'

With his eyes still closed, Tom replies, 'Oh, I'm just checking my car's axle.'

The cop says, 'Well, you'd better check your brakes, too, because your car rolled down the hill a couple of minutes ago.'

Two bored casino dealers are waiting at a craps table. A very attractive blonde woman arrives and bets $20 000 on a single roll of the dice.

She says, 'I hope you don't mind, but I feel much luckier when I'm nude.'

With that she strips from her neck down, rolls the dice and yells, 'Mamma needs new clothes!'

Then she hollers, 'Yes! Yes! I won! I won!'

She jumps up and down and hugs each of the dealers. With that she picks up her winnings and her clothes and quickly departs.

The dealers just stare at each other dumbfounded. Finally, one of them asks, 'What did she roll?'

The other answers, 'I thought you were watching!'

Moral of the story: Not all blondes are dumb.

A man is talking to God and asks, 'God, why did you make women so beautiful?'

'So that you would find them attractive,' God replies.

Then the man asks, 'But why did you have to make them so dumb?'

'So that they would find you attractive!'

Why do men become smarter during sex?
Because they are plugged into a genius.

Why don't women blink during foreplay?
They don't have time.

Why does it take one million sperm to fertilise one egg?
They won't stop for directions.

Why did God put men on earth?
Because a vibrator can't mow the lawn.

What do electric trains and breasts have in common?
They're intended for children, but it's the men who usually end up playing with them.

Why were men given larger brains than dogs?
So they won't hump women's legs at cocktail parties.

Why is a man's pee yellow and his sperm white?
So he can tell if he is coming or going.

How are men like parking spots?
The good ones are always taken and the only ones left are disabled.

It is George the mailman's last day on the job after thirty-five years of carrying the mail through all kinds of weather to the same neighbourhood. When he arrives at the first house on his route he is greeted by the whole family there, who roundly and soundly congratulate him and send him on his way with a tidy gift envelope. At the second house they present him with a box of fine cigars.

The folks at the third house hand him a selection of terrific fishing lures.

At the fourth house, a strikingly beautiful woman in a revealing negligee meets him at the door. She takes him by the hand, gently leads him through the door (which she closes behind him), and leads him up the stairs to the bedroom where she blows his mind with the most passionate love he has ever experienced. When he has had enough they go downstairs, where she fixes him a giant breakfast: eggs, potatoes, ham, sausage, blueberry waffles and freshly squeezed orange juice. When he is truly satisfied she pours him a cup of steaming coffee. As she is pouring, he notices a dollar bill sticking out from under the cup's bottom edge.

'All this was just too wonderful for words,' he says, 'But what's the dollar for?'

'Well,' she says, 'Last night, I told my husband that today would be your last day, and that we should do something special for you. I asked him what to give you. He said, "Screw him. Give him a dollar." The breakfast was my idea.'

The Seven Dwarfs go to the Vatican and are granted an audience with the Pope.

'Dopey, my son,' says the Pope. 'What can I do for you?'

Dopey asks, 'Excuse me, Your Excellency, but are there any dwarf nuns in Rome?'

The Pope wrinkles his brow at this odd question, thinks for a minute and answers, 'No Dopey there are no dwarf nuns in Rome.'

In the background a few of the dwarfs start sniggering. Dopey turns around and gives them a glare, silencing them.

Dopey turns back, 'Your Worship, are there any dwarf nuns in all of Europe?'

The Pope, puzzled now, again thinks for a moment and then answers, 'No Dopey, there are no dwarf nuns in Europe.'

The other dwarfs begin to giggle.

Dopey implores the Pope, 'Mr Pope, are there any dwarf nuns anywhere in the world?'

'I'm sorry, my son, there are no dwarf nuns anywhere in the world.'

The other dwarfs collapse into a heap, rolling around in laughter. They're pounding the floor and tears are rolling down their cheeks as they begin chanting, 'Dopey screwed a penguin! Dopey screwed a penguin!'

Two prostitutes are standing on a street corner, and one says to the other, 'Have you ever been picked up by the fuzz?'

'No, but I've often been swung around by the boobs.'

One morning, Mr Toad wakes up to note with alarm that his penis has turned yellow.

He rushes round to the tree in which Wise Old Owl is nesting, and shows him the affected part.

'No worries,' replies the owl. 'Down the track there, second burrow to the left, you'll find Dr Rabbit. He'll fix you up.'

No sooner has the toad departed than Millie Mouse arrives under Wise Old Owl's tree with a shining pair of pink tits, and seeks the owl's advice.

'Straight down the path,' replies Owl. 'Follow the yellow-dick toad.'

Bob always wanted a pair of authentic cowboy boots. Seeing some on sale one day, he buys them and wears them home, walking proudly. He walks into the bedroom and says to his wife, 'Notice anything different, Bessie?'

Bessie looks him over, 'Nope.'

Bob says excitedly, 'Come on Bessie, take a good look. Notice anything different about me?'

Bessie looks again, 'Nope.'

Frustrated, Bob storms off into the bathroom, undresses, and walks back into the room completely naked except for his boots. Again he asks, a little louder this time, 'Notice anything different?'

Bessie looks up and says, 'Bob, what's different? It's hanging down today, it was hanging down yesterday, and it'll be hanging down again tomorrow.'

Furious, Bob yells, 'And do you know why it is hanging down, Bessie? It's hanging down because it's looking at my new boots!'

Bessie replies, 'Should'a bought a hat, Bob.'

A philosopher is in a bar doing a survey on a group of men, on the topic of happiness. He tells them, 'I can prove to you that the amount of happiness has a relation to the amount of sex you have.' He glances at his audience and sees a man in the right-hand corner, smiling.

'Sir, how often do you have sex?' the philosopher asks.

'Once a month,' the man answers.

Looking for another happy face, he spots a man in the middle, with a bigger smile.

He asks him, 'Sir, how often do you have sex?'

'Once a week,' the man shouts.

Trying to prove his theory further, he sees another man, laughing.

'You seem to be a very happy man. So how often do you have sex?'

'Well…every day,' the happy man answers.

'There, I am right. The amount of happiness is related to the amount of sex you have,' says the philosopher.

Far off at the end of the room, he sees a man with his hands in the air, laughing and jumping with glee. So the philosopher says to him, 'You sure look like a very happy man.'

'Yes, yes, yes,' answers the very happy man.

'So how often do you get to have sex?' the philosopher asks.

The man answers, 'Once a year.'

The puzzled and embarrassed philosopher asks the man, 'What? Then why are you so happy?'

The man starts laughing and jumping and crying out, 'It's tonight, it's tonight!'

Upon arriving home in eager anticipation of getting it on, the husband is met at the door by his sobbing wife.

Tearfully she explains, 'It's the pharmacist. He insulted me terribly this morning on the phone.'

The husband sees he will not be getting any action, so he angrily drives into town to accost the pharmacist and demand an apology.

Before he can say more than a word or two, the pharmacist tells him, 'Now, just a minute – listen to my side of it. This morning the alarm failed to go off, so I was late getting up. I went without breakfast and hurried out to the car but I'll be damned if I didn't lock the house with both house and car keys inside. I had to break a window to get my keys. Driving a little too fast, I got a speeding ticket. Then, about three blocks from the store I got a flat tyre. When I finally got to the store there was a bunch of people waiting for me to open up. I got the store opened and started waiting on these people, and all the time the darn phone was ringing its head off. Then

I had to break a roll of coins against the cash register drawer to make change, and they spilled all over the floor. I got down on my hands and knees to pick up the coins – the phone still ringing – when I came up I cracked my head on the open cash drawer, which made me stagger back against a showcase with a bunch of perfume bottles on it, and half of them hit the floor and broke. The phone was still ringing with no let up, and I finally got back to answer it.

It was your wife. She wanted to know how to use a rectal thermometer. Well, Mister, I told her!'

Two eggs have just been married and are on their honeymoon. While they are sitting on the bed making out, the female egg pushes the male egg away and says, 'I just have to go to the bathroom. I'll be back in a minute,' and off she goes.

Five minutes later the male egg sees his sexy wife walk out in a slinky egglige, running her hands up and down her smooth, oval body. Instantly, the male egg slaps his hands on the top of his head, covering it completely. The female egg looks at him and asks what he is doing.

He replies, 'The last time I was this hard, someone cracked me on the head with a spoon.'

A small tourist hotel was buzzing with gossip about an afternoon wedding where the groom was 95 and the bride was 22.

The groom looked pretty feeble and it was said that the wedding night might kill him, as his bride was a healthy, energetic young woman.

But the next morning, the bride came down the main staircase slowly, step by step, hanging onto the banister for dear life.

When she finally managed to reach the front desk the clerk asked with concern, 'What happened? You look like you've been wrestling an alligator!'

The bride leaned on the counter and groaned, 'Oh God! When he told me he'd been saving up for 95 years, I thought he meant his money!'

A man returns from the doctor and tells his wife that the doctor has told him he has only twenty-four hours to live. Given this prognosis, the man asks his wife for sex. Naturally, she agrees, and they make love.

About six hours later, the husband goes to his wife and says, 'Honey, you know I now have only eighteen hours to live. Could we please do it one more time?'

Of course, the wife agrees, and they do it again. Later, as the man gets into bed, he looks at his watch and realises that he now has only eight hours left.

He touches his wife's shoulder and asks, 'Honey, please… just one more time before I die.'

She says, 'Of course, Dear,' and they make love for the third time.

After this session, the wife rolls over and falls asleep. The man, however, worries about his impending death. He tosses and turns until he's down to four more hours. He taps his wife, who rouses.

'Honey, I only have four more hours. Do you think we could…'

At this point the wife sits up and says, 'Listen, I have to get up in the morning. You don't!'

Jim and Joe often go to the beach to pick up women. Unfortunately, Joe never has any luck, while Jim never fails.

One day, Joe asks Jim the secret of his success. Jim promises to tell Joe, so long as Joe keeps it to himself.

After Joe agrees, Jim says, 'You see the fruit and vegetable shop over the road? Well, every time I come to the beach I buy a potato and put it in my swimming trunks. When the women see it they come running from miles around.'

Joe says, 'That's easy. I can do that.'

The next day, Joe goes over to the shop and picks out the biggest, most perfectly shaped potato he can find. He then goes into the changing room and slips it into his swimming trunks.

As he walks out onto the beach he immediately notices that women begin to take notice of him.

'It's working!' he thinks.

But soon he begins to realise that they are not looking interested but rather upset, almost disgusted, by the sight of him. He rushes over to Jim and asks, 'Jim, what's the problem? Why isn't it working?'

Jim takes one look and says, 'Because you're supposed to put the potato in the front!'

A couple had been married for ten years. Every time they made love the husband always insisted on turning off the light.

Now that ten years had passed, the wife felt this was ridiculous. She decided to break her husband out of this strange habit.

So one night, while they were in the middle of a wild, screaming session, she turned on the light. She looked down to see her husband holding a massive battery-operated vibrator.

'You impotent bastard!' she screamed, 'How could you lie to me all these years?!'

The husband looks her straight in the eyes and says calmly: 'OK, I'll explain the toy, you explain the kids.'

RELIGION

A guy goes to hell and is met by the devil who explains that the punishments of the inmates are changed every thousand years and he is to select his first punishment. The first room has a young guy on the wall being whipped. The new guy is not keen on this and asks to see the next room.

The next room has a middle-aged guy being tortured with fire.

The new guy immediately asks to see the third room. It has a really old guy chained to the wall getting a blow job from a gorgeous blonde. The guy jumps at the chance and selects that room.

The devil walks into the room taps the blonde on the shoulder and says, 'OK, you can stop now. You've been relieved.'

God is just about done creating the universe. He has a couple of left-over things in his bag of creations, so he stops by to visit Adam and Eve in the Garden of Eden. He tells the couple that one of the things he has to give away is the ability to stand up and pee.

'It's a very handy thing,' God tells the couple, who he finds hanging around under an apple tree. 'I was wondering if either one of you wanted that ability?'

Adam pops a cork. He jumps up and begs, 'Oh, give that to me! I'd love to be able to do that! It seems the sort of thing a man should do. Oh please, oh please, oh please, let me have that ability. I'd be so great! When I'm working in the garden or naming the animals, I could just let it rip, I'd be so cool. Oh please, God, let it be me who you give that gift to, let me stand and pee, oh please!'

On and on he goes like an excited little boy. Eve just smiles and shakes her head at the display. She tells God that if Adam really wants it so badly, and it sure seems to be the sort of thing that will make him happy, she really doesn't mind if Adam is the one given the ability to stand up and pee. And so God gives Adam this gift. And it is…well, good.

'Fine,' God says, looking back into his bag of left-over gifts. 'What's left here for you Eve? Oh yes, multiple orgasms.'

A minister dies and is waiting in line at the pearly gates. Ahead of him is a guy who's dressed in sunglasses, a loud shirt, leather jacket and jeans.

St Peter addresses this guy, 'Who are you, so that I may know whether or not to admit you to the kingdom of heaven?'

The guy replies, 'I'm Joe Cohen, taxi-driver.'

St Peter consults his list. He smiles and says to the taxi-driver, 'Take this silken robe and golden staff and enter the kingdom of heaven.'

The taxi-driver goes into heaven with his robe and staff, and it's the minister's turn.

He stands erect and booms out, 'I am Joseph Snow, pastor of Saint Mary's for the last forty-three years.'

St Peter consults his list. He says to the minister, 'Take this cotton robe and wooden staff and enter the kingdom of heaven.'

'Just a minute,' says the minister. 'That man was a taxi-driver and he gets a silken robe and golden staff. How can this be?'

'Up here, we work by results,' says St Peter. 'While you preached, people slept; while he drove, people prayed.'

A married woman is having an affair. Whenever her lover comes over, she puts her nine-year-old son in the closet. One day the woman hears a car in the driveway and, thinking it's her husband, puts her lover in the closet as well.

Inside the closet, the little boy says, 'It's dark in here, isn't it?'

'Yes it is,' the man replies.

'You wanna buy a baseball?' the little boy asks.

'No thanks,' the man replies.

'I think you do want to buy a baseball,' the little extortionist continues.

'OK. How much?' the man replies after considering the position he is in.

'Twenty-five dollars,' the little boy replies.

'Twenty-five dollars?' the man says incredulously, but complies to protect his position.

The following week, the lover is visiting the woman again when she hears a car in the driveway and again places him in the closet with the little boy.

'It's dark in here, isn't it?' the boy starts off.

'Yes it is,' replies the man.

'Wanna buy a baseball glove?' the little boy asks.

'OK. How much?' the hiding lover responds, acknowledging his disadvantage.

'Fifty dollars,' the boy replies and the transaction is completed.

The next weekend, the little boy's father says, 'Hey, son. Go get your ball and glove and we'll play some catch.'

'I can't. I sold them,' replies the little boy.

'How much did you get for them?' asks the father, expecting to hear the profit in terms of lizards and candy.

'Seventy-five dollars,' the little boy says.

'Seventy-five dollars? That's thievery! I'm taking you to church right now. You must confess your sin and ask for forgiveness,' the father says as he hauls the child away.

At the church, the little boy goes into the confessional, draws the curtain, sits down, and says, 'It's dark in here, isn't it?'

'Don't you start that shit in here,' the priest says.

A guy dies and reports immediately at the gates of heaven and St Peter says, 'In checking our records, I find that you have never done anything outstanding enough to get you into heaven.'

'What do you mean?' the guy asks. 'What about when I came to the aid of the little old man who was being pushed around by those motorcycle thugs?'

Obviously impressed, St Peter looks through the record books again. Finding nothing, he says, 'You did that?'

The guy says, 'Yes, I kicked over a couple of bikes and told them to pick on someone their own size.'

St Peter is puzzled. He says, 'There is absolutely no record of it. When did it happen?'

'Oh, about ten minutes ago.'

Four nuns all die together. They are lined up at the pearly gates being asked a series of questions by St Peter.

The last question asked is, 'Have you ever touched a penis?'

The first nun replies, 'Once, with the tip of my finger.'

St Peter tells her to dip her finger in holy water, then she can pass into heaven.

The second nun replies, 'Once, I held one in my hand.'

St Peter tells her to place her hand into holy water, then she can pass into heaven.

Suddenly, the nun that's standing fourth in line pushes ahead of the nun who had been third in line. St Peter asks her why she has done such a thing.

She replies, 'St Peter, if you think I'm going to gargle that holy water after she sits her arse in it, you're crazy.'

Four priests board a train for a long journey to a church council conference. Shortly into the trip, one priest says, 'Well, we've all worked together for many years, but don't really know one another. I suggest we tell each other one of our sins to get better acquainted.'

They look nervously at each other but nod OK.

The first priest says, 'Since I suggested it, I'll go first. With me it's the drink. Once a year I take off my collar and go out of town to a pub and drink myself blind for a few days. Get it out of my system.'

They all look at each other again nervously, but the next priest slowly starts, 'Well, with me, it's the gambling. Periodically, I nick the money out of the poor box and go to the races. Spend it all! But I get it out of my system.'

The third, who is really nervous now, reluctantly says, 'This is very difficult. My sin is worse. I take off my collar and go into the red light district, pick out a lass, and spend a week in the saddle. But I really get it out of my system.'

They all look at the fourth priest, waiting, but he doesn't say anything.

One of the others speaks up, 'Come now, we've all told our innermost faults. It's your turn.'

He looks at the others and starts hesitantly, 'Well, I'm an inveterate gossip, and I can't wait to get off this train!'

A little girl is doing a report on her family tree.

'Mummy, how did I get here?' she asks.

Her mother replies, 'God sent you, sweetie.'

'And did God send you too, mummy?'

'Yes, darling, he did.'

'And daddy and grandma and grandpa and their mums and dads, too?'

'Yes, honey, all of them, too.'

The child shakes her head in disbelief.

'Then you're telling me there's been no sex in this family for over 200 years? No wonder everyone is so grumpy.'

A man is driving down a deserted stretch of highway when he notices a sign out of the corner of his eye.

It reads: 'Sisters of Mercy House of Prostitution – 10 km.'

He thinks it is just a figment of his imagination and drives on without a second thought. Soon, he sees another sign which says: 'Sisters of Mercy House of Prostitution – 5 km.'

He realises that these signs are for real. Then he drives past a third sign saying: 'Sisters of Mercy House of Prostitution – Next Right.'

His curiosity gets the better of him and he pulls into the drive. On the far side of the parking lot is a sombre stone building with a small sign next to the door reading: 'Sisters of Mercy'.

He climbs the steps and rings the bell. The door is answered by a nun in a long black habit who asks, 'What may we do for you, my son?'

He answers, 'I saw your signs along the highway, and was interested in possibly doing business.'

'Very well, my son. Please follow me.'

He is led through many winding passages and is soon quite disoriented. The nun stops at a closed door, and tells the man, 'Please knock on this door.'

He does as he is told and the door is answered by another nun in a long habit, holding a tin cup. This nun instructs, 'Please place $50 in the cup, then go through the large wooden door at the end of this hallway.'

He gets $50 out of his wallet and places it in the second nun's cup. He trots eagerly down the hall and slips through the door, pulling it shut behind him. As the door locks behind him, he finds himself back in the parking lot, facing another small sign: 'Go in Peace, You Have Just Been Screwed by the Sisters of Mercy.'

Jesus is strolling through heaven when he sees an old man sitting on a cloud, staring disconsolately into the distance.

'Old man,' says Jesus, 'this is heaven! Why are you so sad?'

The old man doesn't bother to turn as he says, 'I've been looking for my son and haven't been able to find him.'

Jesus says, 'Tell me about it.'

'Well,' says the old man, still gazing at the sunlit horizon, 'on earth I was a carpenter, and one day my son went away. I never heard from him again, and I was hoping I'd find him here, in heaven.'

His heart pounding suddenly in his chest, Jesus bends over the old man and says, 'Father?'

The old man turns and cries, 'Pinocchio?'

One morning the Pope awakes in his bed chamber in the Vatican. To his surprise, he notices that he has woken up with a massive erection. Perplexed, he calls on his personal physician.

'Doctor, this should not be possible,' he says, 'I'm the Pope, and I'm celibate! I haven't had one of these for thirty years!'

The doctor replies, 'Well, father, this is a natural phenomenon for all men, and it will happen even to you from time to time.'

The Pope exclaims, 'But you must do something about this. I have Mass in an hour, and this thing isn't going away.'

The doctor replies, 'You have two options. Either I can administer an injection to your penis to make the problem go away, which will hurt and make you feel ill, or you can make love to a woman.'

The Pope says, 'No, I do not want the injection, so get me a nun. But there are three considerations. First, she must be blind so she cannot see who does this thing to her. Second, she must be deaf so she cannot hear who does this thing to her. Third, she's gotta have really big tits.'

A wealthy farmer went to church one Sunday. After the service he said to the priest, 'Father, that was a damned good sermon you gave, damned good!'

'I'm happy you liked it,' said the priest. 'But I wish you wouldn't use those terms in expressing yourself.'

'I can't help it,' said the rich farmer. 'I still think it was a damned good sermon. In fact, I liked it so much I put $100 in the collection basket.'

'Holy shit, that's great!' replied the priest.

A couple have two little boys, aged eight and ten, who are excessively mischievous. The two are always getting into trouble and their parents are sure that if any mischief occurs in their town, their two young sons are in some way involved. The parents are at their wits' end as to what to do about their sons' behaviour. The mother has heard that a clergyman in town has been successful in disciplining children in the past, so she asks her husband if he thinks they should send the boys to speak with the clergyman.

The husband says, 'We might as well. We need to do something before I really lose my temper.'

The clergyman agrees to speak with the boys, but asks to see them individually. The eight-year-old goes to meet with him first.

The clergyman sits the boy down and asks him sternly, 'Where is God?'

The boy makes no response, so the clergyman repeats the question in an even sterner tone, 'Where is God?'

Again the boy makes no attempt to answer, so the clergyman raises his voice even more and shakes his finger in the boy's face, 'Where is God!'

At that the boy bolts from the room and runs directly home slamming himself in his closet.

His older brother follows him into the closet and says, 'What happened?'

The younger brother replies, 'We are in big trouble this time. God is missing. And they think we did it!'

God is talking to one of his angels.

He says, 'Boy, I just created a 24-hour period of alternating light and darkness on Earth.'

The angel says, 'What are you going to do now?'
God says, 'Call it a day.'

Jesus came across an adulteress crouching in a corner with a crowd around her preparing to stone her to death. He stopped the crowd and said, 'Let he who is without sin cast the first stone.'

Suddenly a woman at the back of the crowd fired off a stone at the adulteress.

Jesus looked over and said, 'Mother! Sometimes you really piss me off!'

Two nuns are riding their rickety old bikes down the bumpy back streets of Rome late one summer afternoon. It starts getting quite dark and the two nuns are a little nervous. The younger nun steers her bicycle closer to the older nun and says, 'You know, I've never come this way before.' The older nun nods her head knowingly and says, 'It's the cobblestones.'

Two nuns are ordered to paint a room that is going to be redecorated in the convent for a visit by the pope. The last instruction from Mother Superior is that they must not get so much as a drop of paint on their habits. After conferring about this for a while, the two nuns decide to lock the door of the room, strip off their habits, and paint in the nude.

In the middle of the project, there is a knock at the door.

'Who is it?' calls one of the nuns.

'It's the blind man,' replies a voice from the other side of the door.

The two nuns look at each other and shrug, deciding that no harm can come from letting a blind man into the room. They open the door.

'Nice tits,' says the man, 'where do you want the blinds?'

Three women die together in an accident and go to heaven. When they get there, St Peter says, 'We only have one rule here in heaven, don't step on the ducks.'

So they enter heaven, and sure enough, there are ducks all over the place. It is almost impossible not to step on a duck, and although they try their best to avoid them, the first woman accidentally steps on one. Along comes St Peter with the ugliest man she ever saw.

St Peter chains them together and says, 'Your punishment for stepping on a duck is to spend eternity chained to this ugly man!'

The next day, the second woman steps accidentally on a duck, and along comes St Peter, who doesn't miss a thing, and with him is another extremely ugly man. He chains them together with the same admonishment he gave to the first woman.

The third woman has observed all this and, not wanting to be chained for all eternity to an ugly man, is very, very careful where she steps. She manages to go months without stepping on any ducks, but one day St Peter comes up to her with the most handsome man she has ever laid eyes on. Very tall, long eyelashes, muscular and thin. St Peter chains them together without saying a word.

The woman remarks, 'I wonder what I did to deserve being chained to you for all of eternity?'

The guy says, 'I don't know about you, but I stepped on a duck!'

ON THE FARM

An old cowboy sits in a saloon and orders a drink. A young woman sits down next to him.

'Excuse me, are you a real cowboy?' she asks.

'Well, I break colts, work cows, go to rodeos, bail hay, doctor calves, clean my barn and work on tractors, so I guess that makes me a cowboy through and through! What do you do, sweetheart?'

The woman replies, 'I'm a lesbian. I spend all day thinking about women. As soon as I wake up, I think about women. When I'm having a shower, I think about women. When I drive my car, I think about women. I even think about women when I eat. It seems that everything makes me think of women.'

They sat drinking in silence.

A few minutes later, a man sat down on the other side of the old cowboy and asked, 'Are you a real cowboy?'

He replied, 'I always thought I was, but I just found out I'm a lesbian.'

A horse is stumbling home from the pub after a solid night of drinking when he falls into a huge hole by the side of the road. No matter how hard he tries, he cannot climb out. He starts to panic, knowing that Farmer Brown will be furious if he is not at work on time. Along comes a chicken.

'Hey chicken!' cries the horse. 'You have to help me. I'm pissed and I gotta get home for work or the farmer will drag me to the glue factory.'

The chick looks at the horse, then at the hole, and finally tells the horse that he is far too small to haul the horse up. He has no other choice but to leave him there. The horse suddenly has an idea.

'I've got it! Go home and get the farmer's Porsche, drive over here and tie a rope to the bumper and drag me out of this hole and home.'

The chicken agrees and sure enough, it works. A few days later, the horse is walking by the same bar and past the same hole when he finds the chicken pissed out of his head and clucking around aimlessly at the bottom of the hole.

'Hey, horse!' the chicken shouts. 'You gotta help me! I can't make it out and the farmer will chop my neck if I'm not home in the morning to give him eggs.'

The horse looks at the chicken and at the hole and admits that although he owes him a huge favour, he couldn't possibly get down to pick him up. So the chicken tells the horse to go home and get the farmer's Porsche and come back and get him. But the horse tells the chicken that while it sounds like a great idea, he's far too big to fit in the car.

The chicken starts to cry and the horse feels so badly that he begins to rack his brains to find a solution to help out the chicken, who, after all, had saved his arse. Finally, he has an idea. He stands over the hole and lets down his huge horse cock. He tells the chicken to grab on and proceeds to pull him out of the hole. The chicken gets home on time and all is well.

The moral of this story is: If you're hung like a horse; you don't need a Porsche to pick up chicks.

In a classroom of third graders, the teacher says to the kids, 'Today, class, we will be telling stories that have a moral to them.'

She explains what a moral to a story is and asks for volunteers. Little Suzie raises her hand.

'I live on a farm and we have a chicken that laid twelve eggs, we were excited to have twelve more chickens but only six of them hatched,' she says.

'That's a good story, now what is the moral?' asks the teacher.

'Don't count your chickens before they hatch.'

'Very good Suzie, anyone else?'

'Yes teacher,' says Ralphie. 'I was carrying some eggs I bought for my mum in my bicycle basket one day and I crashed my bike and all the eggs broke.'

'That's a nice story, what is the moral?'

'Don't put all your eggs in one basket.'

'Very good Ralphie, anyone else?'

'Yes teacher,' says little Johnny. 'My Aunt Karen is in the army and when she was in the Gulf War, she parachuted down with only a gun, twenty bullets, a knife, and a six-pack of beer. On her way down, she drank the six pack. When she landed, she shot twenty Iraqis and killed ten of them with her knife.'

'Very interesting, Johnny, what is the moral to your story?'

'Don't screw with Aunt Karen when she's drunk.'

A ventriloquist goes for a walk in the country and sees a farmer sitting on his porch with his dog. The ventriloquist asks the farmer if he can talk to the dog.

'Dogs don't talk,' the farmer tells him.

'Well, can I try?'

'Sure, go ahead. Though you're wasting your time.'

'Hey dog, how's it goin'?' asks the ventriloquist.

'Doin' all right,' replies the dog.

The farmer is shocked, while the ventriloquist proceeds to trick the farmer.

'Is this your owner?' the ventriloquist asks, pointing at the farmer.

'Yep,' the dog replies.

'How's he treat you?'

'Real good. He walks me twice a day, feeds me great food, and takes me to the lake once a week to play.'

Next, the ventriloquist asks if he can speak to the farmer's horse.

'Horses don't talk,' the farmer says.

Again, the ventriloquist insists until the farmer agrees.

'Hey horse, how's it goin'?' the ventriloquist asks.

'Cool,' the horse replies.

The farmer looks even more astonished than when the dog spoke.

'Is this your owner?' the ventriloquist asks, pointing at the farmer.

'Yep,' the horse replies.

'How's he treat you?'

'Pretty good, thanks for asking. He rides me regularly, brushes me down often, and keeps me in the barn to protect me from the elements.'

The ventriloquist then turns to the farmer again and asks, 'Mind if I talk to your sheep?'

The farmer gesticulates wildly and is hardly able to talk. Nevertheless, he manages to blurt out, 'Them sheep ain't nothin' but liars, every darned one of 'em!'

An extraordinarily handsome man decided he has the God-given responsibility to marry the perfect woman so they can produce children beyond comparison. With this as his mission he begins searching for the perfect woman. After a diligent, but fruitless, search up and down the east coast, he starts to head west. Shortly thereafter he meets a farmer who has three stunningly gorgeous daughters that positively take his breath away. So he explains his mission to the farmer, asking for permission to marry one of them.

The farmer simply replies, 'They're all lookin' to get married, so you came to the right place. Look them over and select the one you want.'

The man dates the first daughter. The next day the farmer asks for the man's opinion.

'Well,' says the man. 'She's just a weeeeee bit, not that you can hardly notice, but pigeon-toed.'

The farmer nods and suggests the man date one of the other girls; so the man goes out with the second daughter.

The next day, the farmer again asks how things went.

'Well,' the man replies, 'She's just a weeeee bit, not that you can hardly tell, cross-eyed.'

The farmer nods and suggests he date the third girl to see if things are any better. So he does.

The next morning the man rushes in exclaiming, 'She's perfect, just perfect! She's the one I want to marry.'

So they are wed right away. Eventually, a baby is born. When the man visits the nursery he is horrified. The baby is the ugliest, most pathetic human you can imagine. He rushes to his father-in-law asking how such a thing could happen considering the parents.

'Well,' explains the farmer. 'She was just a weeeee bit, not that you could hardly tell, pregnant when you met her.'

What do cow pies and cowgirls have in common?
The older they are, the easier they are to pick up.

A cowboy dies and, as he was a bad fellow, he goes straight down to hell. When he gets down there the devil is waiting. The devil says, 'You have three choices for ways to spend your eternity. Do you pick door number one, two or three?'

The cowboy says, 'Let me check what's behind door number one.'

The door opens and he sees hundreds of people standing on their heads on a wood floor.

'I don't want this,' he says, 'let's try door number two.'

The door opens and he sees hundreds of people standing on their heads on a hard cement floor.

'Woah! I don't want to spend the rest of my life like that! What's behind door number three?'

The door opens and he sees hundreds of people drinking coffee, and having a good time, but they are all up to their knees in horse poo.

'I'm a cowboy, I'm used to horse dung. I'll go with door number three,' he says.

The devil hands him a cup of coffee and introduces him to the crowd and leaves him to it.

After ten minutes, the devil comes back in and says, 'Coffee break's over. Everybody back on their heads.'

A farmer was involved in a terrible road accident with a large truck. He ended up in court fighting for a big compensation claim.

'I understand you're claiming damages for the injuries you're supposed to have suffered?' said the counsel for the insurance company.

'Yes, that's right,' replied the farmer.

'You claim you were injured in the accident, yet I have a signed police statement that says when the attending police officer asked you how you were feeling, you replied, "I've never felt better in my life." Is that true?'

'Yeah, but –'

'A simple yes or no will suffice.'

'Yes,' replied the farmer quietly.

Then it was the turn of the farmer's counsel to ask the questions.

'Please tell the court the exact circumstance of events following the accident when you made your statement of health,' his lawyer said.

'Certainly,' replied the farmer. 'After the accident my horse was thrashing around with a broken leg and my poor old dog was howling in pain. This cop comes along, takes one look at my horse and shoots him dead. Then he goes over to my dog, looks at him and shoots him dead too. Then he comes straight over to me, with his gun still smoking, and asks me how I was feeling. Now, mate, what the hell would you have said to him?'

LEISURE TIME

Two hunters are out in the woods when one of them collapses. He doesn't seem to be breathing and his eyes are glazed. The other guy whips out his mobile phone and calls the emergency services.

He gasps, 'My friend is dead! What can I do?'

The operator says, 'Calm down, I can help. First, let's make sure he's dead.'

There's a silence, then a shot is heard.

Back on the phone, the guy says, 'OK, now what?'

Two hunters are out looking for pheasant when they come upon the local farmer's daughter, sitting naked on a fence, sunning herself.

The first hunter asks, 'Are you game?'

She replies, 'I sure am, Honey!'

So the second hunter shoots her.

Two hunters are dragging their dead deer back to their car. Another hunter approaches pulling his along too. 'Hey, I don't want to tell you how to do something, but I can tell you that it's much easier if you drag the deer in the other direction. Then the antlers won't dig into the ground.'

After the third hunter leaves, the two decide to try it.

A little while later one hunter says to the other, 'You know, that guy was right. This is a lot easier!'

'Yeah, but we're getting farther from the truck,' the other adds.

Bob and Earl were two fishermen who lived for their sport. They fished at every opportunity and watched all the fishing shows on television. They pored over every magazine article on fishing and discussed tactics on how to win the major fishing competitions. They even agreed that whoever died first would try to come back and tell the other if there was fishing in heaven.

One summer night, Bob passed away in his sleep after coming in from a big day out fishing. He had had a good day and so he died happy. A few nights later, his buddy Earl awoke to the sound of Bob's voice coming from beyond.

'Bob, is that you?' Earl exclaimed. 'This is unbelievable! So tell me, is there fishing in heaven?'

'Well, I have some good news and some bad news for you. Which do you want to hear first?'

'Tell me the good news first.'

'The good news is that yes, there is fishing in heaven.'

'Oh, that is wonderful! So what could possibly be the bad news?'

'You're coming out fishing with me tomorrow night.'

Mrs Pete Monaghan came into the newsroom to pay for her husband's obituary. She was told by the kindly newsman that it was a dollar a word and he remembered Pete and wasn't it too bad about him passing away. She thanked him for his kind words and bemoaned the fact that she only had two dollars. But she wrote out the obituary, 'Pete died.'

The newsman said he thought old Pete deserved more and he'd give her three more words at no charge. Mrs Pete Monaghan thanked him profusely and rewrote the obituary: 'Pete died. Boat for sale'

WHY FISHING IS BETTER THAN SEX

- When you go fishing and you catch something, that's good. If you're having sex and you catch something, that's bad.

- Fish don't compare you to other fishermen and don't want to know how many other fish you have caught.

- In fishing you lie about the one that got away. With sex you lie about the one you caught.

- You can catch and release a fish without having to lie and promise to still be friends after you've let it go.

- You don't have to change your line to keep catching fish.

- You can catch a fish on a twenty-cent night crawler. If you want to catch a woman you're talking at least dinner and a movie.
- Fish don't mind if you fall asleep while you're fishing.

GOLF IS BETTER THAN SEX BECAUSE

- If you damage a ball it is easy to replace it with a new one.
- The lay is always different.
- A hole in one is applauded.

GOLFER: Well, I have never played this badly before!

CADDY: I didn't realise you had played before, sir.

GOLFER: Notice any improvement today, Jimmy?

CADDY: Yes, ma'am. You've had your hair done.

GOLFER: Caddy, do you think it is a sin to play golf on Sunday?

CADDY: The way you play, sir, it's a crime any day of the week!

GOLFER: I'd move heaven and earth to be able to break 100 on this course.

CADDY: Try heaven. You've already moved a fair amount of earth.

A man came home and was greeted by his wife dressed only in very sexy underwear and holding a couple of ropes.

'Tie me up,' she said, 'and you can do anything you want.'

So he tied her up and went to play golf.

The antenatal class is in full swing with pregnant women and their partners learning how to breathe properly and how to provide support at birth.

At one point, the teacher announces, 'Ladies, exercise is good for you. Walking is especially beneficial. And, gentlemen, it wouldn't hurt you to take the time to go walking with your partner!'

One man raises his arm to ask a question.

'Yes?' asks the teacher.

'Is it all right if she carries a golf bag while we walk?'

A young woman has been taking golf lessons. She has just started playing her first round of golf when she suffers a bee sting. The pain is so intense that she decides to return to the clubhouse.

Her golf pro sees her come into the clubhouse and asks, 'Why are you back in so early? What's wrong?'

'I was stung by a bee.'

'Where?' he asks.

'Between the first and second hole,' she replies.

He nods knowingly and says, 'Apparently your stance is too wide.'

A very attractive couple are playing golf and the wife hits a beautiful, long shot – right through the window of a house.

Horrified, the couple go to the house to apologise and offer to pay for the damage. A tall, handsome man answers the door.

'Come in! Come in!' he cries.

The couple, embarrassed by the smiling welcome, confess to breaking the window.

'I know, I know,' says the man. 'And I'm pleased you did.' The couple exchange confused glances.

'You see that urn?' the man continues, pointing to what had been an antique masterpiece but is now lying in pieces on the floor.

'Oh no!' the wife cries. 'Don't tell me I've broken that too!'

'Don't be worried,' says the man. 'You see I've been in that urn for years and years. I'm a genie and you have set me free.'

The couple just stare at him in amazement.

'Now,' says the genie. 'I have the power to grant three wishes. Why don't we share them. One each.'

Turning to the wife he says, 'What is your greatest wish?'

'Well,' she says hesitantly, 'I would like to think I could have peace of mind and a quiet, calm life forever.'

'Done!' says the genie. 'And what about you Sir?'

The husband doesn't waste a minute to reply. 'I would like to have enough money to live a life of total luxury, to be able to afford expensive cars, take super cruises and live in the best stateroom on the ship, and have a grand house – with servants.'

'Done!'

The husband looks extremely pleased and asks the genie his wish.

The genie looks slightly embarrassed. 'That's rather delicate actually.' He turns to the wife and says, 'Do you mind if I speak to your husband alone for a moment?'

'Not at all,' she says.

The genie takes the husband aside. 'You have a very beautiful wife. I know I shouldn't ask this but my wish would be to spend just one night alone with her. What do you think?'

'Well I'm not sure,' says the husband. 'I'd have to discuss it with her and see how she feels about it.'

'Naturally,' says the genie.

The couple give the proposition some thought and then the wife says that the genie is, after all, giving them a lifetime of peace, security and luxury. Maybe it isn't really too big an ask – just one night.

'If you're OK with it, I am,' says the husband.

'Actually,' says the wife with a smile, 'he's not unattractive you know. I'm really quite happy to oblige.'

The genie and the wife have a wonderful night together and the next morning the genie says, 'I really want to thank you. I've had a marvellous time with you and I think you quite enjoyed it too.'

'Oh I did,' says the wife.

'Please', the genie says, 'Do you mind if I ask you just one question? How old is your husband?'

'Forty-three.'

At this the genie raises his eyebrows. 'And he still believes in genies?'

EATING OUT

Waiter, there's a fly in my soup!
    Force of habit, Sir. Our chef used to be a tailor.
    Waiter, there's a fly in my soup!
Couldn't be, Sir. The cook used them all in the raisin bread.
Waiter, there is a fly in my soup!
Sorry Sir, maybe I missed it when I removed the other three.
Waiter, there's a dead fly in my soup!
What do you expect for $5 – a live one?
Waiter, waiter, there's a bee in my soup.
Yes Sir, it's the fly's day off.
Waiter, this coffee tastes like dirt!
Yes Sir, that's because it was only ground this morning.

A waiter brings a customer the steak he ordered, with his thumb over the meat.
    'Are you crazy?' yells the customer. 'What are you doing with your hand on my steak?'
    'What?' asks the waiter. 'You want it to fall on the floor again?'
    How many waiters does it take to change a light bulb?
    None, a burned out bulb can't catch a waiter's eye.
    'What flavours of ice cream do you have?' inquires the customer.
    'Vanilla, strawberry and chocolate,' answers the new waitress in a hoarse whisper.
    Trying to be sympathetic, the customer asks, 'Do you have laryngitis?'
    'No,' replies the new waitress with some effort, 'just…erm …vanilla, strawberry and chocolate.'

GROWING OLD GRACEFULLY

On hearing that her grandfather had passed away, Mary went straight over to comfort her ninety-five-year-old grandmother.

'How did he die?' Mary asked, as she embraced her little old grandmother.

'He had a heart attack while we were making love on Sunday morning.'

Horrified, Mary told her grandmother, 'Surely having sex when you are nearly one hundred years old is asking for trouble!'

'Oh no, dear,' replied her grandmother. 'Many years ago, when we started getting older, we figured out the best time to do it was when the church bells started to ring. It was just the right rhythm. Nice and slow and even. He went in on the Ding and out on the Dong.'

She wiped away a tear and then continued, 'And if it wasn't for that damned ice cream truck, he'd still be alive today!'

An eighty-five-year-old man marries a beautiful twenty-five-year-old woman. Because her new husband is so old the woman decides that on their wedding night they should have separate suites. She is concerned that the old fellow could over-exert himself.

After the festivities she prepares herself for bed and for the knock on the door she is expecting. Sure enough the knock comes and there is her groom ready for action. They start making love and all goes well. He then leaves her room and she prepares to go to sleep for the night.

After a few minutes there's a knock on the door and there is the old man again, ready for more action. Somewhat surprised she consents to further sex, which is again successful. When it is over, the octogenarian bids her a fond goodnight and leaves.

She is very tired now and is close to sleep when, again, there is a knock at the door. There he is, fresh as a twenty-five-year-old and ready for more action. Once again they make love.

As they're lying alongside each other afterwards, the young bride says to him, 'I am really impressed that a guy your age has enough juice to go for it three times. I've been with guys less than half your age that were only good for one…you're great.'

The man looks confused, and turns to her and says, 'Have I been in here before?'

After forty years of marriage, Frankenstein and the Bride of Frankenstein come to a stand-still in their love life. Each night Frankenstein comes home from work, eats his dinner, and sits in front of the television until he falls asleep.

Dissatisfied with this arrangement, the Bride decides to see a therapist.

'He's never in the mood,' complains the Bride.

'Try a romantic candlelit dinner,' suggests the therapist.

The next day, the Bride returns to the therapist with a frown on her face.

'He's still not in the mood,' she complains.

'This time,' the therapist recommends, 'try something more seductive. Put on some sexy lingerie and lure him into the bedroom.'

But the Bride returns to the therapist the following day complaining that her monster of a husband is still not in the mood.

As a final piece of advice, the therapist says, 'You should try to recreate the moment that first sparked your romance.'

The next day the Bride returns with a huge grin on her face.

'Thank you so much,' she says to the therapist. 'Last night, I forced Frankenstein to come outside in the middle of the lightning storm. And right there, in our backyard, he made love to me like it was our very first time.'

'Making love in a lightening storm put him in the mood?' asks the therapist.

'Well,' says the Bride of Frankenstein, 'I tied a kite to his penis.'

Two old ladies are walking through a museum and get separated.

When they run into each other later the first old lady says, 'My! Did you see that statue of the naked man back there?'

The second old lady replies, 'Yes! I was absolutely shocked! How can they display such a thing! My gosh the penis on it was so large!'

And the first old lady blurts out, 'And cold, too!'

For her 100th birthday, the family decided to have a party for Grandma. Everybody was in the backyard, and Grandma sat in her wheelchair in the middle of it all. She couldn't speak very well, but she could write notes when she needed to communicate.

As the party got going, Grandma slowly started leaning to the right, so some family members grabbed her, straightened her up, and stuffed pillows on her right side.

A short time later, she started slowly leaning to the left, so again the family members grabbed her and stuffed pillows on her left.

Soon Grandma started leaning forward, so the family members again grabbed her and then tied a pillowcase around her waist to hold her up.

A grandson, who arrived late, came up to Grandma, kissed her on the cheek and said, 'Happy birthday, Grandma! Are you having a good time? How are they treating you?'

Grandma took out her little notepad and slowly wrote a note to the grandson: They won't let me fart.

A couple have been married for fifty years. They are sitting at the breakfast table one morning when the old gentleman says to his wife, 'Just think, honey, we've been married for fifty years.'

'Yeah,' she replies, 'just think, fifty years ago we were sitting here at this breakfast table together.'

'I know,' the old man says, 'we were probably sitting here naked as jaybirds fifty years ago.'

'Well,' Granny snickers, 'what do you say…should we get naked?'

So the two strip to the buff and sit down at the table.

'You know, honey,' the little old lady whispers, 'my nipples are as hot for you today as they were fifty years ago.'

'I'm not surprised,' replies Gramps. 'One's in your coffee and the other is in your porridge.'

A police car pulls up in front of grandma's house and grandpa gets out. The polite policeman explains to grandma that the poor gentleman was lost in the park and couldn't find his way home.

'Oh dear,' says grandma. 'You've been going to that park for over thirty years. How could you get lost?'

Leaning close to grandma, so that the policeman can't hear, grandpa whispers, 'I wasn't lost. I was just too tired to walk home.'

An old lady and an old man are sitting in their retirement home.

The man turns to the woman and says, 'I bet you can't tell how old I am.'

She says, 'OK.'

She then unzips his fly, feels around for a while and finally says, 'You're eighty-three.'

'That's amazing!' the man exclaims. 'How did you know?'

She replies, 'You told me yesterday.'

An eighty-five-year-old man visits his doctor to get a sperm count. The man is given a jar and told to bring back a sample. The next day he returns to the doctor with an empty jar.

'What happened?' asks the doctor.

'Well,' the old man starts,' I asked my wife for help. She tried with her right hand, then she tried with her left – nothing. Then she tried with her mouth, first with her teeth in, then with her teeth out, still nothing. We even called Evelyn, the lady next door, but still nothing.'

The doctor bursts out, 'You asked your neighbour?'

'Yep, no matter what we tried we couldn't get that damn jar open.'

An old lady in a nursing home is wheeling up and down the halls in her wheelchair making sounds like she's driving a car.

As she's going down the hall, an old man jumps out of a room and says, 'Excuse me Ma'am but you were speeding. Can I see your driver's licence?'

She digs around in her purse a little, pulls out a candy wrapper, and hands it to him. He looks it over, gives her a warning and sends her on her way. Up and down the halls she goes again.

Again, the same old man jumps out of a room and says, 'Excuse me Ma'am but I saw you cross over the centre line back there. Can I see your registration please?'

She digs around in her purse, pulls out a store receipt and hands it to him. He looks it over, gives her another warning and sends her on her way. She zooms off again up and down the halls weaving all over. As she comes to the old man's room again, he jumps out. He's stark naked and has an erection.

The old lady in the wheelchair looks up and says, 'Oh, no, not the breathalyser again!'

A ninety-year-old man is having his annual check-up. The doctor asks him how he is feeling.

'I've got a hot eighteen-year-old wife who's pregnant with my child. What do you think about that?'

The Doctor considers this, and then says, 'Let me tell you a story. I know a guy who just loves hunting. But one day he's in a bit of a hurry to get out there and he accidentally grabs his umbrella instead of his gun. So he's walking in the forest near a creek and he suddenly spots a beaver. He raises up his umbrella, points it at the beaver and squeezes the handle. And boom! The beaver drops dead in front of him.'

'That's impossible!' says the old man in disbelief. 'Someone else must have shot that beaver!'

The doctor says, 'My point exactly.'

A guy goes to his grandmother's house and takes one of his friends with him. While he's talking to his grandmother, his friend starts eating the peanuts on the coffee table and finishes them off.

As they are leaving, the friend says, 'Thanks for the peanuts.'

She says, 'Yeah, since I lost my dentures I can only suck the chocolate off 'em.'

An older lady is lonely, and decides that she needs a pet to keep her company. So off to the pet shop she goes.

Forlornly, she searches but nothing seems to catch her interest, except one ugly frog. As she walks by the barrel he is in, he looks up and winks at her.

He whispers, 'I'm lonely too, buy me and you won't be sorry.'

The old lady thinks, why not? She hasn't found anything else.

So, she buys the frog and takes it to her car.

Driving down the road the frog whispers to her, 'Kiss me, you won't be sorry.'

So, the old lady thinks what the hell, and kisses the frog.

Immediately the frog turns into an absolutely gorgeous, sexy, handsome, young prince. Then the prince kisses her back, and you know what the old lady turns into?

The first motel she can find.

BEING OVER 60 HAS ITS ADVANTAGES

- No one expects you to run into a burning building.
- People call at 9 p.m. and ask, 'Did I wake you?'
- People no longer view you as a hypochondriac.
- There's nothing left to learn the hard way.

- You can eat dinner at 4 p.m.
- You can live without sex, but not without glasses.
- You enjoy hearing about other people's operations.
- You get into heated arguments about pension plans.
- You have a party and the neighbours don't even realise it.
- You quit trying to hold your stomach in, no matter who walks into the room.
- You sing along with the elevator music.
- Your investment in health insurance is finally beginning to pay off.
- Your joints are more accurate weather gauges than the Bureau of Meteorology.
- Your secrets are safe with your friends because they can't remember them either.

Two old ladies were outside their nursing home having a smoke, when it started to rain. One of the ladies pulled out a condom, cut off the end, put it over her cigarette, and continued smoking.

'What's that?' asked the other lady.

'A condom.'

'Where'd you get it?'

'You can get them at any drugstore.'

The next day, the second lady hobbled into the local drugstore and announced to the pharmacist that she wanted to buy a package of condoms. The guy looked at her kind of strangely (she was, after all, in her 80s), but politely asked what brand she preferred.

'Doesn't matter,' she replied, 'as long as it fits a Camel.'

An old maid lives in a tiny village. In spite of her old age, she is still a virgin and she is very proud of it. She knows her last days are getting closer, so she tells the local undertaker that she wants the following inscription on her tombstone: 'Born as a virgin, lived as a virgin, died as a virgin.'

Not long after, the old maid dies peacefully, and the undertaker tells his men what the lady has said. The men go to carve it in, but as the lazy no-goods they are, they think the inscription is unnecessarily long.

They simply write: 'Returned unopened'.

The wealthy old gentleman and his wife were celebrating their 35th wedding anniversary and their three grown sons joined them for dinner. The old man was rather irritated when he discovered none of the boys had bothered to bring a gift, and after the meal, he drew them aside.

'You're all grown men,' he said, 'and old enough to hear this. Your mother and I have never been legally married.'

'What?' gasped one of the sons. 'Do you mean to say we're all bastards?'

'Yes,' snapped the old man, 'and cheap ones, too!'

A little boy is helping his grandfather with the gardening. The boy discovers an earthworm trying to get into its hole but struggling.

He says, 'Grandpa, I bet I can put that worm back in the hole.'

The grandfather replies, 'I'll bet you five dollars you can't. It's too soft and limp to put back in that little hole.'

So the little boy runs into the house and comes back with a can of hairspray. He sprays the worm until it is straight and stiff as a board. Then he pushes the worm into the hole.

The grandfather hands the boy five dollars, grabs the hairspray, and runs into the house. Half an hour later, the grandfather comes back out and hands the little boy another five dollars.

'But Grandpa, you already gave me five dollars.'

The grandfather replies, 'I know. That's from your grandma.'

Eighty-year-old Jessie bursts into the rec room of the men's retirement home. She holds her clenched fist in the air and announces, 'Anyone who can guess what's in my hand can have sex with me tonight!'

An elderly gentleman in the rear shouts out, 'An elephant?'

Jessie thinks a minute and says, 'Close enough.'

The drugs that we use when we're ailing
    Go by different names for retailing
    Tylenol's acetamenophen.
Advil's Ibuprofen.
And Viagra is Mycoxafailing.

A woman saw a little wrinkled up man rocking in a chair on his porch.

'I couldn't help noticing how happy you look. What's your secret for a happy life?' she asked him.

'I smoke three packs of cigarettes a day. I also drink a case of whisky a week, eat lots of fatty foods, and never ever take any exercise.'

'That's amazing. Exactly how old are you?'

'Twenty-six.'

A SAD TALE

My nookie days are over,
my pilot light is out.
What used to be my sex appeal,
is now my water spout.
Time was when, of its own accords,
from my trousers it would spring.
But now I have a full time job,
just to find the blasted thing.
It used to be embarrassing,
the way it would behave.
For every single morning,
it would stand and watch me shave.
But now as old age approaches,
it sure gives me the blues.
To see it hang its withered head,
and watch me tie my shoes.

THE BELL CURVE OF LIFE

At age 4 success is not peeing in your pants.
At age 10 success is making your own meals.
At age 12 success is having friends.
At age 18 success is having a driver's licence.
At age 20 success is having sex.
At age 35 success is having money.
At age 50 success is having money.
At age 60 success is having sex.
At age 70 success is having a driver's licence.
At age 75 success is having friends.
At age 80 success is making your own meals.
At age 85 success is not peeing in your pants.

A ninety-year-old woman decides that she's seen and done everything, and the time has come to depart from this world.

After considering various methods of doing away with herself, she comes to the conclusion that the quickest and surest method is to shoot herself through the heart. The trouble is, she isn't certain exactly where her heart is, so she phones her doctor and asks him. He tells her that her heart is located two inches above her left nipple. So she shoots herself in the left kneecap.

B ecky is on her deathbed with her husband, John, maintaining a steady vigil by her side. As he holds her fragile hand, his warm tears run silently down his face, splashing onto her face, and rousing her from her slumber. She looked up and her pale lips began to move slightly.

'My darling John,' she whispers.

'Hush, my love,' he says. 'Go back to sleep. Shhh. Don't talk.'

But she is insistent. 'John,' she says in her tired voice. 'I have to talk. I have something I must confess to you.'

'There's nothing to confess,' replies the weeping John. 'It's all right. Everything's all right, go to sleep now.'

'No, no. I must die in peace, John,' she says. 'I slept with your brother, your best friend and your father.'

John musters a pained smile and strokes her hand.

'Hush now Becky, don't torment yourself. I know all about it,' he says. 'Why do you think I poisoned you?'

Two men have a dad who is turning eighty. The old guy's been a widower for fifteen years, so the sons decide to get him a prostitute for the night as a surprise. The young and curvy woman shows up at the old guy's door, wearing a sexy outfit. When he opens the door she says seductively, 'Are you ready for some super sex?'

The old man looks her up and down, then sighs deeply, and replies, 'I'll take the soup please.'

EDUCATION

For weeks a six-year-old lad keeps telling his first-grade teacher about the baby brother or sister that is expected at his house. One day his mother allows the boy to feel the movements of the unborn child in her belly. The six-year-old is obviously impressed, but makes no comment. Furthermore, he stops telling his teacher about the impending event.

The teacher finally sits the boy down and says, 'Tommy, whatever has become of that baby brother or sister you were expecting at home?'

Tommy bursts into tears and confesses, 'I think Mummy ate it!'

Johnny is always saying that he is too smart for the first grade.

He thinks he should at least be in the third grade. One day, his teacher has had enough. She takes Johnny to the principal's office and explains Johnny's request, while Johnny waits in the outer office. The principal tells Johnny's teacher that he will give the boy a test and if Johnny fails to answer any of the special questions he is to go back to the first grade and behave. The teacher agrees.

Johnny is brought into the room. The principal tells Johnny his terms and Johnny agrees.

'What is three times three?' asks the principal.

'Nine,' replies Johnny.

'What's six times six?'

'Thirty-six.'

'What's nine times nine?'

'Eighty-one.'

And so it goes with every question the principal thinks a third-grader should know. Johnny appears to have a strong case. The principal tells the teacher, 'I think Johnny can go on to the third grade.'

The teacher, knowing Little Johnny's tendency towards sexual wisecracks, says to the principal, 'Let me ask him some questions before we make that decision.'

The principal and Johnny both agree, Johnny with a sly look on his face. The teacher begins by asking, 'What does a cow have four of that I have only two of?'

'Legs,' Johnny answers.

'What is in your pants that you have but I don't have?' asks the teacher.

The principal's eyes open wide! Before he can stop Johnny's expected answer, he says, 'Pockets.'

The principal breathes a sigh of relief and tells the teacher, 'I think we should put Johnny in the fifth grade. I missed the last two questions myself!'

An autopsy lecturer is giving an introductory lecture to a class of students. Standing over a corpse, he addresses the class.

'There are two things you need to make a career in medical forensics. First, you must have no fear.'

Having said that, he shoves his finger up the corpse's arsehole then licks it.

'Now you must do the same,' he tells the class.

After a couple of minutes of uneasy silence, the class do as instructed.

'Second,' the lecturer continues, 'you must have an acute sense of observation. For instance, how many of you noticed that I put my middle finger up this man's anus, but licked my index finger?'

On the first day of uni, the Dean addresses the students, pointing out some of the rules. 'The female dormitory will be out-of-bounds for all male students, and the male dormitory for all female students. Anybody caught breaking this rule will be fined $20 the first time. Anybody caught breaking this rule the second time will be fined $60. Being caught a third time will cost you a fine of $180. Are there any questions?'

A male student in the crowd inquires, 'How much for a season pass?'

BUSINESS IS BUSINESS

One morning, the postman came to deliver a parcel. He stopped in front of the house, only to find a small boy at the door swigging from a beer bottle, smoking a cigar, with his arm around what appeared to be a prostitute. Surprised, the postman asked the boy if his parents were home.

'What the hell do you think?'

A very successful lawyer parked his brand-new BMW in front of his office, ready to show it off to his colleagues. As he got out, a truck passed too close and completely tore the door off the driver's side. The counsellor immediately grabbed his mobile phone, dialled emergency, and within minutes a policeman pulled up. Before the officer had a chance to ask any questions, the lawyer started screaming hysterically.

His BMW, which he had just picked up the day before, was now completely ruined and would never be the same, no matter what the panel-beater did to it.

When the lawyer finally wound down from his ranting and raving, the officer shook his head in disgust and disbelief. 'I can't believe how materialistic you lawyers are,' he said.

'You are so focused on your possessions that you don't notice anything else.'

'How can you say such a thing?' asked the lawyer.

'Don't you know that your left arm is missing from the elbow down? It must have been torn off when the truck hit you.'

'Ahhh!' screamed the lawyer. 'Where's my Rolex?'

The stockbroker is nervous about being in prison because his cellmate looks like a real thug.

'Don't worry,' the gruff-looking fellow says, 'I'm in here for a white-collar crime too.'

'Well, that's a relief,' sighs the stockbroker. 'I was sent to prison for fraud and insider trading.'

'Oh nothing fancy like that for me,' grins the convict. 'I just murdered a couple of priests.'

A man is in a VIP airport lounge en route to Seattle. He is meeting with a very important client who is also flying to Seattle but she is running a bit late. While waiting, he notices Bill Gates sitting in a chair enjoying a cognac. Being a forward type of guy, the man approaches Bill Gates and introduces himself. He explains to Gates that he is conducting some very important business and that he would really appreciate it if Gates could throw a quick 'Hello Paul' at the man while he is with his client.

Gates agrees. Ten minutes later, while the man is conversing with his client, he feels a tap on his shoulder. It is Gates. The man turns around and looks up at him.

Bill Gates says, 'Hi Paul, what's happening?'

The man replies, 'Piss off, Bill, I'm in a meeting.'

The Pope and a lawyer find themselves together before the pearly gates. After a little polite small talk, St Peter shows up to usher them to their new heavenly station. After passing out wings, harps, halos and such, St Peter shows them to their new lodgings. Peter brings them down on the front lawn of a huge palatial estate with all sorts of lavish trappings. This, Peter announces, is where the lawyer will be spending eternity.

'Holy Mary,' the Pope thinks. 'If he's getting a place like this, I can hardly wait to see my heavenly reward!'

Peter leads the way but the landscape below begins to appear more and more mundane until they finally land on a street lined with dull brownstone houses. Pete indicates that the third stairs on the left will take the Pope to his new domicile and turns to leave, wishing the Pope the best.

The Pope is quite taken aback and cries out, 'Hey Peter! What's the deal here? You put that lawyer in a beautiful estate home and I, spiritual leader of the whole world, end up in this dive?'

'Look here old fellow, this street is practically encrusted with spiritual leaders from many times and from many religions. We're putting you here with them so you can all get together and discuss dogma and philosophy. That other guy gets an elegant estate, because he's the first lawyer ever to make it up here.'

Smith goes to see his supervisor in the front office.

'Boss,' he says, 'we're doing some heavy house-cleaning at home tomorrow and my wife needs me to help with the attic and the garage, moving and hauling stuff.'

'We're short-handed, Smith,' the boss replies. 'I can't give you the day off.'

'Thanks, boss,' says Smith, 'I knew I could count on you!'

The boss walked into the office one morning not realising his zipper was down and gaping.

His assistant walked up to him and said, 'This morning when you left your house, did you close your garage door?'

'Of course,' he replied, and walked into his office puzzled by her question.

When he sat down, he noticed his fly was open, and zipped it up. He then understood his assistant's question about his 'garage door'.

He headed out for a cup of coffee and paused by her desk, winked, and asked, 'When my garage door was open, did you see my Hummer parked in there?'

She smiled and said, 'No, I didn't. All I saw was an old minivan with two flat tyres.'

A man walks up to a woman in his office and tells her that her hair smells nice. The woman immediately goes into her supervisor's office and tells him that she wants to file a sexual harassment suit and explains why.

The supervisor is puzzled and says, 'What's wrong with your co-worker telling you that your hair smells nice?'

The woman replies, 'He's a midget.'

A blonde, a brunette and a redhead all work at the same office for a female boss who always goes home early.

'Hey, girls,' says the brunette, 'let's go home early tomorrow. She'll never know.'

So the next day, they all leave right after the boss does. The brunette gets some extra gardening done, the redhead goes to a bar, and the blonde goes home to find her husband having sex with the female boss! She quietly sneaks out of the house and comes back at her normal time.

'That was fun,' says the brunette. 'We should do it again sometime.'

'No way,' says the blonde. 'I almost got caught.'

10 EXCUSES TO USE WHEN CAUGHT NAPPING AT YOUR DESK

1 ….in the Lord Jesus' name, Amen.

2 They told me at the blood bank this might happen.

3 Damn! Why did you interrupt me? I had almost worked out a solution to our biggest problem.

4 I was doing yoga exercises to relieve work-related stress.

5 Someone must've put decaf in the wrong pot.

6 I was testing my keyboard for drool resistance.

7 This is just a 15-minute powernap, as described in that time management course you sent me.

8 I wasn't sleeping! I was meditating on the mission statement and envisioning a new paradigm.

9 The coffee machine is broken.

10 Whew! Guess I left the top off the liquid paper! You got here just in time!

HOW TO ANNOY THE HELL OUT OF EVERYONE ELSE AT YOUR WORKPLACE

- Page yourself over the intercom. Don't disguise your voice.

- Find out where your boss shops and buy exactly the same outfits. Wear them one day after your boss does. This is especially effective if your boss is of a different gender than you.

- Make up nicknames for all your co-workers and refer to them only by these names, eg 'That's a good point, Sparky', or 'No, I'm sorry, but I'm going to have to disagree with you there, Cha-Cha'.

- Highlight your shoes. Tell people you haven't lost them as much since you did this.

- Hang mosquito netting around your cubicle. When you emerge to get a coffee or a printout or whatever, slap yourself randomly the whole way.

- Put a chair facing a printer. Sit there all day and tell people you're waiting for your document.

- Every time someone asks you to do something, anything, ask them if they want fries with that.

Marty woke up after the annual office Christmas party with a terrible headache, completely unable to recall the events of the evening.

He slowly made his way downstairs, where his wife gave him a headache tablet and some water.

'Darling,' he said, 'please tell me what happened last night. Was it as bad as I think?'

'Even worse,' she replied scornfully. 'You made a complete idiot of yourself. You succeeded in being rude to the entire board of directors and you insulted the chairman of the company to his face.'

Marty slouched with his head in his hands, 'He's an asshole anyway. Piss on him.'

'You did, actually. And he fired you.'

'Well, screw him!' said Marty.

'I did. You're back at work on Monday.'

A site foreman had 10 very lazy men working for him, so one day he decided to trick them into doing some work for a change.

'I've got a really easy job today for the laziest one among you,' he announced. 'Will the laziest man please put his hand up?'

Nine hands went up.

'Why didn't you put your hand up?' he asked the 10th man.

'Too much trouble,' came the reply.

A man was eating in a restaurant and he dropped his spoon. The waiter was immediately at his table and took another spoon out of his pocket and gave it to the man. The man thanked him, and took a sip of his soup and then asked, 'Excuse me, but why do all the waiters have spoons in their pockets?'

The waiter said, 'Well sir, a time and motion survey in our restaurant showed that one in four customers drop their spoon just like you, so we always have a spare spoon on hand so we can give it to the customer so that he is not eating with the dirty one. It saves time as the waiter does not have to go back to the kitchen to retrieve a clean spoon. The management prides itself in the efficiency of the staff.'

Just as the waiter was about to walk back to the kitchen, the man noticed that there was a string hanging from his fly and the man said, 'Excuse me but why do you and all the other waiters have a string hanging out of your flies?'

The waiter said, 'Well sir, a survey in our restaurant showed that the waiters can save time and serve more customers if we do not wash our hands after using the toilet. So we use the string tied to our penises to pull it out of our trousers so we don't get our hands dirty.'

Then the man took another sip of his soup and replied, 'That's all very well, but how do you get it back in again?'

'Well I don't know about the others,' replied the waiter. 'But personally, I use the spoon.'

Why did the Auditor cross the road?
Because he did it last year!
Who was the world's first accountant?
Adam. He turned a leaf and made an entry!

Why does the government jail people for theft?
It doesn't want any competition.

Why was the sailor buried at sea?
Because he was dead.

AMUSING ANSWERING MACHINE MESSAGES

Twinkle, twinkle little star
How we wonder who you are.
Leave a message at the beep.
We'll call back before you sleep.
Twinkle, twinkle little star,
Betcha you're wondering where we are.

Now I lay me down to sleep;
Leave a message at the beep.
If I should die before I wake,
Remember to erase the tape.

No, No! Not that! Anything but that! Not the beep!
No! Please! Not the beep! Anything but the beep!
AAAAIIIIEEEEEEEEEEEE!

Hi! John's answering machine is broken. This is his refrigerator. Please speak very slowly, and I'll stick your message to myself with one of these magnets.

Hello, this is Ron's toaster. Ron's new answering machine is in the shop for repairs, so please leave your message when the toast is done.

Hi. Now you say something.

If you are a burglar, then we're probably at home cleaning our weapons right now and can't come to the phone. Otherwise, we aren't home, and it's safe to leave a message.

Greetings, you have reached the Sixth Sense Detective Agency. We know who you are and what you want, so at the sound of the tone, just hang up.

(In a Darth Vader voice) Speak, worm!

A small business owner has two employees, Jack and Jill. Business is bad and the business owner has to lay one of them off but is having a hard time deciding which one.

He decides that the first one to leave for lunch is the one that he'll lay off.

But both of them stay and eat at their desks.

Then he decides that the first one to leave work at the end of the day will be the one he fires. They both get up and leave at the same time.

He has to let one of them go. Which one? He decides on Jill.

The owner walks out to Jill's car as she is about to get in and says, 'Jill, I am trying to decide whether to lay you or Jack off. What do you think?'

Jill says, 'You'd better just jack off. I'm already late for an appointment.'

An engineer had an exceptional gift for fixing all things mechanical. After serving his company loyally for over 30 years, he happily retired. A few years later the company contacted him regarding an impossible problem they were having with one of their multi-million dollar machines. They had tried everything and everyone else to get the machine fixed, but to no avail.

In desperation, they called on the retired engineer who had solved so many of their problems in the past. The engineer reluctantly took the challenge. He spent a day studying the huge machine.

At the end of the day, he marked a small 'x' in chalk on a particular component of the machine and proudly stated, 'This is where your problem is'.

The part was replaced and the machine worked perfectly again. The company received a bill for $50,000 from the engineer for his service. They demanded an itemised accounting of his charges. The engineer responded briefly: One chalk mark: $1. Knowing where to put it: $49,999.

It was paid in full and the engineer retired again in peace.

When Picasso was tender in years
He considered some other careers
When he read a reportage
Of an imminent shortage
Of models with eyes in their ears.

One day a farmer called up an engineer, a physicist and a mathematician and asked them to fence off the largest possible area with the least amount of fence.

The engineer made the fence in a circle and proclaimed that he had the most efficient design.

The physicist made a long, straight line and proclaimed, 'We can assume the length is infinite.'

He pointed out that fencing off half of the earth was certainly the most efficient way to do it.

The mathematician built a tiny fence around himself and said, 'I declare myself to be on the outside.'

A mortician who practised in Fife
    Made love to the corpse of his wife.
    'How could I know, Judge?
She was cold, did not budge
Just the same as she'd acted in life.'

An engineer, an accountant, a chemist and a bureaucrat were bragging about how smart their dogs were. To settle the argument they agreed to put their dogs through their paces.

The engineer called to his dog, 'T-square, do your stuff.'

The dog took out paper and pen and drew a circle, a square and a triangle. Everyone was suitably impressed.

The accountant called, 'Taxation, do your stuff.'

The pooch went to the kitchen, got a dozen cookies and made four stacks of three. The others nodded their surprise.

So the chemist called, 'Beaker, do your stuff.'

The dog went to the fridge for a bottle of milk, got a 250 ml glass and poured exactly 200 ml without spilling a drop.

Everyone agreed that was great.

Finally it was the bureaucrat's turn, 'Coffee-Break, do your stuff!'

Coffee-Break ate the cookies, drank the milk, chewed the paper, said he injured his mouth doing so, filed a claim for unsafe working conditions, put in for worker's compensation and took extended sick leave.

If an accountant's wife cannot sleep, what does she say? 'Darling, could you tell me about your work?'

1 Gary Wales, assistant programmer, can always be found
2 hard at work at his desk. He works independently, without
3 wasting company time talking to colleagues. Gary never

4 thinks twice about assisting his colleagues, and always

5 finishes given assignments on time. He takes extended

6 measures to complete his work, sometimes skipping coffee

7 breaks. Gary is a dedicated individual who has no

8 vanity in spite of his high accomplishments and profound

9 knowledge in his field. I believe that Gary can be

10 classed as an asset employee, a man who cannot be

11 dispensed with. Consequently, I recommend that Gary be

12 promoted to executive management; a proposal will be

13 executed as soon as possible.

Addendum

That moron was looking over my shoulder while I wrote the report. Kindly re-read only the odd numbered lines.

In the prime of her career, a world-famous painter started to lose her eyesight. Fearful that she might lose her career, she went to see the best eye surgeon in the world. After several weeks of delicate surgery and therapy, her eyesight was restored.

The painter was so grateful that she decided to show her gratitude by repainting the doctor's office. Part of her mural included a gigantic eye on one wall. When she had finished her work, she held a press conference to unveil the mural.

During the press conference, one reporter noticed the eye on the wall.

'What was your first reaction upon seeing your newly painted office, especially that large eye on the wall?' he asked the doctor.

'My first thought was: Thank God I'm not a gynaecologist.'

Four surgeons are taking a coffee break and are discussing their work.

The first says, 'I think accountants are the easiest to operate on. You open them up and everything inside is numbered.'

The second says, 'I think librarians are the easiest to operate on. You open them up and everything inside is in alphabetical order.'

The third says, 'I like to operate on electricians. You open them up and everything inside is colour-coded.'

The fourth one says, 'I like to operate on lawyers. They're heartless, spineless, gutless, and their head and their arse are interchangeable.'

What do lawyers use for birth control?
Their personalities.

What can a goose do that a duck can't, and a lawyer should?
Stick his bill up his arse.

A lawyer and a blonde are sitting next to each other on a long flight. The lawyer leans over to her and asks if she would like to play a fun game. The blonde just wants to take a nap, so she politely declines and rolls over to the window to catch a few winks. The lawyer persists and explains that the game is really easy and a lot of fun.

He explains, 'I ask you a question, and if you don't know the answer, you pay me $5, and vice-versa.'

Again, she politely declines and tries to get some sleep. The lawyer, now somewhat agitated, says, 'OK, if you don't know the answer you pay me $5, and if I don't know the answer, I will pay you $500.' He reckons that since she is a blonde that he will easily win the match. This offer catches the blonde's attention and, realising that there will probably be no end to this torment unless she plays, agrees to the game.

The lawyer asks the first question. 'What's the distance from the earth to the moon?'

The blonde doesn't say a word, reaches in to her purse, pulls out a $5 note and hands it to the lawyer. Now, it's the blonde's turn.

She asks the lawyer, 'What goes up a hill with three legs, and comes down with four?'

The lawyer looks at her with a puzzled look. He takes out his laptop computer and searches all his references. He taps into the air-phone with his modem and searches the Net and the Library of Congress. Frustrated, he sends emails to all his co-workers and friends. All to no avail. After over an hour, he wakes the blonde and hands her $500. The blonde politely takes the $500 and turns away to get back to sleep.

The lawyer, who is more than a little miffed, wakes the blonde and asks, 'Well, so what is the answer?'

Without a word, the blonde reaches into her purse, hands the lawyer $5, and goes back to sleep.

There are three types of people: those who can count and those who can't.

Three engineers and three accountants are travelling by train to a conference. At the station, the three accountants each buy a ticket and watch as the three engineers only buy one ticket. 'How are three people going to travel on only one ticket?' asks an accountant.

'Watch and you'll see,' answers an engineer.

They all board the train. The accountants take their respective seats but all three engineers cram into a rest room and close the door behind them. Shortly after the train has departed, the conductor comes around collecting tickets.

He knocks on the toilet door and says, 'Tickets, please!'

The door opens just a crack and a single arm emerges with a ticket in hand. The conductor takes it and moves on. The accountants see this and agree it is a clever idea.

So after the conference, the accountants decide to copy the engineers on the return trip and save some money. When they get to the station, they buy one ticket for the return trip. To their astonishment, the engineers don't buy a ticket at all.

'How are you going to travel without a ticket?' asks one perplexed accountant.

'Watch and you'll see,' answers an engineer.

When they board the train all three accountants cram into a toilet and the three engineers cram into another one nearby.

The train departs. Shortly afterward, one of the engineers leaves the toilet and walks over to the toilet where the accountants are hiding.

The engineer knocks on the door and says, 'Tickets, please!'

An accountant is having a hard time sleeping and goes to see his doctor. 'Doctor, I just can't get to sleep at night.'

'Have you tried counting sheep?'

'That's the problem. I make a mistake and then spend three hours trying to find it.'

What's the difference between a lawyer and a rooster?

When a rooster wakes up in the morning, its primal urge is to cluck defiance.

How can you tell when a lawyer is lying?

His lips are moving.

How many lawyers does it take to roof a house?
Depends on how thin you slice them.

What would happen if you locked a zombie in a room full of lawyers?
He would starve to death.

What do you call a lawyer gone bad?
Your honour.

What do you call 5000 dead lawyers at the bottom of the ocean?
A good start!

What do you have when a lawyer is buried up to his neck in sand?
A shortage of sand.

One day, a teacher, a garbage collector and a lawyer all die and go to heaven. St Peter is there but is having a bad day since heaven is getting crowded. When they get to the gate, St Peter informs them that there will be a test to get into heaven – they each have to answer a single question.

To the teacher, he says, 'What was the name of the ship that crashed into the iceberg and sank with all its passengers?'

The teacher thinks for a second and then replies, 'That would be the *Titanic*, right?'

St Peter lets him through the gate. Then he turns to the garbage man, and, thinking that heaven doesn't really need all the stink that this guy would bring into it, decides to make the question a little harder, 'How many people died on the ship?'

The garbage man guesses, '1228.'

'That happens to be right; go ahead.'

St Peter turns to the lawyer, 'Name them.'

Two tigers are stalking through a jungle in Asia. Suddenly, the one to the rear reaches out with his tongue, and licks the posterior of the tiger in front of him.

The startled front tiger turns and says, 'Cut it out.'

The rear tiger apologises, and they continue onward.

About five minutes later, it happens again.

The front tiger turns, growling, 'I said stop it.'

The rear tiger again apologises, and they continue.

Another five minutes pass, and again the front tiger feels the unwanted tongue.

The front tiger turns, giving the rear tiger a ferocious glare, and angrily hisses, 'What is it with you?'

The rear tiger replies, 'I'm sorry. I really didn't mean to offend you. But I just ate a lawyer and I'm trying to get the taste out of my mouth!'

What's the difference between a lawyer and a trampoline? You take off your shoes to jump on a trampoline.

What's the difference between a dead skunk in the road and a dead lawyer in the road?

There are skid marks in front of the skunk.

TOILET HUMOUR

Barry and Joe are drinking buddies who work as aeroplane mechanics in Melbourne. One day the airport is closed due to a storm.

Barry says, 'I wish we had something to drink!'

Joe replies, 'Me too. I heard you can drink jet fuel if you want a buzz. Want to try it?'

So they pour themselves some high-octane fuel and get completely trashed.

The next morning Barry wakes up and is surprised at how good he feels. No hangover and no other side effects.

The phone rings, and it's Joe.

Joe says, 'Hey, how are you feeling this morning?'

'I feel great. How about you?'

Joe says, 'I feel great, too. I don't even have a hangover!'

Barry replies, 'This jet fuel is great! We should to do this more often.'

'Yeah, well there's just one thing…'

'What's that?'

'Have you farted yet?'

'No…'

'Well, don't, 'cause I'm in Canberra!'

A man has a serious problem. Every time he takes a step, he farts. He goes to the doctor and when he walks in, 'Parp! Fumph! Toot! Poop!' go his bowels.

He sits down and the doctor tells him to walk across the room. He walks across the room and again his arse explodes with each stride, 'Parp! Fumph! Toot! Poop!' He walks back to his seat, 'Toot! Fumph! Parp! Poop! Rumble.'

'I know what I'm going to do!' says the doctor.

He goes to his cupboard and brings out a giant pole with a great big hook on the end of it.

The fellow looks in horror and says, 'Jeez, Doc, what the hell are you gonna do with that?'

'I'm going to open the window, of course. This place stinks!'

Three lunatics were walking down the road when they came across a huge pile of shit.

The first loony put his eye in it and said, 'Look's like shit'.

The next one put his nose in it and said, 'Smell's like shit'.

The last one put his tongue in it and said, 'Taste's like shit'.

They all looked at each other and said, 'Lucky we did not stand in it!'

Two beggars, Seamus and Niall, were walking along the road at dusk. Being the more amateur of the two, Niall complained loudly, 'I'm famished! How will we get something to eat this night?'

'Worry not,' said Seamus, 'I'll show you how it's done.'

As they approached a farmhouse, he picked up a dried cow pat from the field and went to the door. He knocked on the door, and the missus answered.

'Yes?' she said.

'Forgive me missus,' begged Seamus, 'I am but a humble beggar with nought to eat but this dried old cow pat. Could I trouble you for some salt to go with it?'

'Why that's no fit meal for a man,' the woman exclaimed.

'Come in here and sit down, I'll feed you proper.'

A half hour later, Seamus emerged from the house stuffed with lamb and potatoes and smiling ear to ear.

'Wow,' shouted Niall, 'I can do that!'

He ran to the next farmhouse, grabbing his own cow pat along the way. He knocked on the door, and the missus answered.

'Forgive me missus,' he begged, 'I am but a humble beggar with nought to eat but this dried-up old cow pat. Could I trouble you for some salt to go with it?'

'Snakes alive,' she cried 'that's no fit meal for a man. That thing's all horrible and dried up. Go on out back and get yourself a fresh one.'

A very attractive young lady was sitting in a fine restaurant one night. She was waiting for her special date and she wanted to make sure everything was perfect. As she bent down in her chair to get the mirror from her purse, she accidentally farted quite loudly just as the waiter walked by. She sat upright, embarrassed and red faced, knowing that everyone in the place had heard her.

To cover her embarrassment she turned to the waiter and demanded loudly, 'Stop that!'

'Sure lady, which way is it headed?' said the waiter.

A guy goes to pick up his date. She's still getting ready, so he has to sit in the living room with her parents.

He has a bad case of gas and really needs to relieve some pressure.

Luckily, the dog jumps up on the couch next to him. He decides that he can let a little fart out and if anyone notices they will think that it was the dog.

He farts, and the woman yells, 'Molly! Get down.'

He smiles and thinks, 'Great, they think the dog did it'.

He releases another fart, and the woman again yells for the dog to get down.

This goes on for several more farts.

Finally the woman yells, 'For goodness sake, Molly, get down before he shits on you.'

SOME THINGS TO PONDER ON THE LOO

- If all the world is a stage, where is the audience sitting?
- If all is not lost, where is it?
- If God dropped acid, would he see people?
- What's the speed of dark?
- If you're in hell and mad at someone, where do you tell them to go?
- What happens if you were scared half to death twice?
- How is it possible to have a civil war?
- If only the good die young, what does that say about senior citizens?
- How can you be alone with someone?
- If corn oil comes from corn, where does baby oil come from?
- What do sheep count when they can't get to sleep?
- If it's tourist season, why can't we shoot them?
- Why do they call it instant credit, when it actually means instant debt?
- If we're not supposed to eat late-night snacks, why is there a light in the refrigerator?

- Why is it called a TV set, when you only get one?
- Did God create man before woman because He didn't want any advice?
- Isn't it scary that doctors call what they do 'practice'?
- Why do they sterilise needles for a lethal injection?
- Can a blonde play an AM radio in the evening?
- Why are they called 'apartments', when they're all stuck together?
- Does a heavy voice on the phone mean I should not go to bed with that person?
- How come wrong numbers are never busy?
- If a word in the dictionary was misspelled, how would we know?
- If space is a vacuum, who changes the bags?
- Where do they keep daylight savings time?
- Why do banks charge you an 'insufficient funds' fee when they know you don't have any funds?
- If the No 2 pencil is the most popular why is it still No 2?
- Can a stupid person be a smart-arse?
- Why is the time of day with the slowest traffic called rush hour?
- Since Australians throw rice at weddings, do Asians throw meat pies?
- When God rested on the seventh day, what did He do?
- And if He played golf, did he set a course record?
- If man evolved from monkeys and apes, why are there still monkeys and apes?
- Do they give pilots crash courses in flight school?

- Is killing time a crime?
- When I erase a word with a pencil, where does it go?
- How do you get off a non-stop flight?
- If you're sending someone Styrofoam, what do you pack it in?
- How do you write zero in Roman numerals?
- Can you buy a full chess set in a pawn shop?
- Why is the third hand on a watch called the second hand?
- Why don't people in Australia call the rest of the world 'up over'?
- If all those psychics know the winning lottery numbers, why are they still working for a living?
- How did a fool and his money get together in the first place?
- Why doesn't the fattest man in the world become a goalie?
- How can someone draw a blank?
- Before they invented drawing boards, what did they go back to?
- How come Superman can stop a bullet with his chest but always ducks when someone throws a gun at him?
- Why do we wait till a pig is dead before we cure it?
- When everything is coming your way, are you in the wrong lane?
- If tin whistles are made out of tin, what are fog horns made out of?
- Can vegetarians eat animal crackers?
- Is Santa always jolly because he knows where all the bad girls live?

As a present to himself on his 65th birthday, Scott joins a luxury nudist colony. On his first day he takes off his clothes and starts wandering around.

A gorgeous blonde walks by him and Scott immediately gets an erection. The woman notices his erection, comes over to him smiling and says, 'Sir, did you call for me?'

Scott is embarrassed and replies, 'No, what do you mean?'

'You must be new here,' she replies. 'It's a rule here that if I give you an erection, it implies you called for me.'

Smiling, she then lies down on a towel and pulls Scott towards her. They have passionate sex.

Scott continues exploring the facilities. He enters the sauna, sits down and accidentally farts. Suddenly a huge, hairy man with a massive erection comes out of the steam towards him.

The huge man says, 'Sir, did you call for me?'

Terrified, Scott replies, 'No, what do you mean?'

'You must be new here. It is a rule that when you fart, it implies you called for me.'

The huge man then turns Scott around, bends him over the bench and has passionate sex with him.

Scott runs back to the colony office.

'Here is your card and key back. You can keep the joining fee!'

The naked receptionist says, 'But sir, you've only been here a few hours, surely you've only seen a small fraction of what we have to offer.'

'Listen. I'm 65 years old. I get a hard-on twice a month, but I fart 30 times a day. No thanks.'

MORE THINGS TO PONDER ON THE LOO

- All those who believe in psychokinesis raise my hand.
- Ambition is a poor excuse for not having enough sense to be lazy.
- Beauty is in the eye of the beer holder.
- Black holes are where God divided by zero.
- Corduroy pillows – they're making headlines!
- Drink 'til she's cute, but stop before the wedding.
- Eagles may soar, but weasels don't get sucked into jet engines.
- Energizer Bunny arrested, charged with battery.
- Everyone has a photographic memory, but some don't have any film.
- Excuses are like arses – everyone's got 'em and they all stink.
- For Sale: Parachute. Only used once, never opened, small stain.
- Give a man a free hand and he'll run it all over you.

- How do you tell when you run out of invisible ink?
- I almost had a psychic girlfriend but she left me before we met.
- I couldn't repair your brakes, so I made your horn louder.
- I drive way too fast to worry about cholesterol.
- I intend to live forever – so far, so good.
- I love defenceless animals, especially in good gravy.
- I poured Spot remover on my dog. Now he's gone.
- I used to have an open mind but my brains kept falling out.
- If Barbie is so popular, why do you have to buy her friends?
- If everything seems to be going well, you have obviously overlooked something.
- If I worked as much as others, I would do as little as they do.
- If you ain't making waves, you ain't kicking hard enough!
- If you choke a Smurf, what colour does it turn?
- Join the army, meet interesting people, kill them.
- Laughing stock – cattle with a sense of humour.
- Many people quit looking for work when they find a job.
- Quantum mechanics – the dreams stuff is made of.
- Shin – a device for finding furniture in the dark.
- Support bacteria – they're the only culture some people have.
- The early bird gets the worm, but the second mouse gets the cheese.
- The only substitute for good manners is fast reflexes.
- Wear short sleeves – support your right to bare arms!
- When I'm not in my right mind, my left mind gets pretty crowded.
- Who is General Failure and why is he reading my hard disk?
- Why do psychics have to ask you for your name?

woman has a passion for baked beans. She loves them but unfortunately she has always had a very embarrassing and somewhat lively reaction to them. Then one day she meets a guy and falls in love. When it becomes apparent that they will marry she thinks to herself, 'He is such a sweet and gentle man, I would hate to lose him. I just have to give up beans.'

Some months later her car breaks down on the way home from work. Since she lives in the country, she calls her husband and tells him that she will be late because she has to walk home. On her way she passes a small diner and the odour of the baked beans is more than she can stand. Since she still has miles to walk, she reckons that she will walk off any ill effects by the time she reaches home. So, she stops at the diner and before she knows it, she has consumed three large plates of baked beans. All the way home she farts. Upon arriving home, she feels reasonably sure she can control it.

Her husband seems excited to see her and exclaims delightedly, 'Darling, I have a surprise for dinner tonight.'

He then blindfolds her and leads her to her chair at the table. She seats herself and just as he is about to remove the blindfold, the telephone rings.

He makes her promise not to touch the blindfold until he returns. He then goes to answer the phone. The baked beans she has consumed are still affecting her and the pressure is becoming almost unbearable, so while her husband is out of the room she seizes the opportunity, shifts her weight to one leg and lets it go. It is not only loud, but it smells like a fertiliser truck running over a skunk in front of a pulpwood mill. She takes her napkin and fans the air around her vigorously. Then, she shifts to the other cheek and rips three more, which remind her of cabbage cooking. Keeping her ears tuned to the conversation in the other room, she goes on like this for another ten minutes. When the phone farewells signal the end of her freedom, she fans the air a few more times with her napkin, places it on her lap and folds her hands upon it, smiling contentedly to herself.

She is the picture of innocence when her husband returns. Apologising for taking so long, he asks her if she peeked, and she assures him that she didn't. At this point, he removes the blindfold, and she is surprised.

There are twelve dinner guests seated around the table to wish her a happy birthday.

EVEN MORE THINGS TO PONDER ON THE LOO

- A planetarium puts on all-star shows.
- A plastic surgeon's office is the only place where no one gets offended when you pick your nose.
- If a cow laughed, would milk come out her nose?

- If a no-armed man has a gun, is he armed?
- If a shop is open 24 hours a day, 365 days a year, why are there locks on the doors?
- If a turtle doesn't have a shell, is he homeless or naked?
- If nothing ever sticks to Teflon, how do they make Teflon stick to the pan?
- If swimming is so good for the figure, how then do you explain whales?
- If you cross a four-leaf clover with poison ivy, would you get a rash of good luck?
- If you crossed an electric blanket with a toaster, would you pop out of bed quicker in the morning?
- If you feed gunpowder to a chicken do you get an eggsplosion?
- If you get into a taxi and the driver starts driving backwards, does s/he owe you money?
- If you tied buttered toast to the back of a cat and dropped it from a height, which way would it end up?
- Is it bad luck to be superstitious?
- Is it true that cannibals won't eat clowns because they taste funny?
- Is there another word for synonym?
- Smoking kills, and if you're killed, you've lost a very important part of your life.
- The trouble with most referees is that they don't care who wins.
- What do people in China call their best plates?
- What do you call a male ladybird?

- What was the best thing before sliced bread?
- When dog food is new and improved, who tested it?
- Who says nothing is impossible? Some people do it every day.
- Why didn't Noah swat those two mosquitoes?
- Why doesn't glue stick to the inside of the bottle?
- Why is a carrot more orange than an orange?
- Why is abbreviated such a long word?
- Why is it that when a door is open, it's ajar, yet when a jar is open, it's not a door?
- Why isn't phonetic spelled the way it sounds?
- Why isn't there mouse-flavoured cat food?
- Would a fly without wings be called a walk?

AREN'T KIDS CUTE?

Little Joe sees his daddy's car pass the playground and go into the woods. Curious, he follows the car and sees Daddy and Aunt Susie in a passionate embrace.

Joe finds this exciting and can barely contain himself as he runs home and starts to tell his mother, 'Mummy, Mummy, I was at the playground and Daddy and –'

Mummy tells him to slow down. She wants to hear the story.

So Joe tells her, 'I was at the playground and I saw Daddy go into the woods with Aunt Susie. I went back to look and he was giving Aunt Susie a big kiss, then he helped her take off her shirt, then Aunt Susie helped Daddy take his pants off, then Aunt Susie laid down on the seat, then Daddy –'

At this point, Mummy cuts him off and says, 'Joe, this is such an interesting story, suppose you save the rest of it for dinner. I want to see the look on Daddy's face when you tell it tonight.'

At the dinner table, Mummy asks Joe to tell his story. Joe starts his story, describing the car going into the woods, the undressing, laying down on the seat, and '…then Daddy and Aunt Susie did that same thing that Mummy and Uncle Bill used to do when Daddy was away on his business trip!'

The first-grade teacher is starting a new lesson on multi-syllable words. She thinks it will be a good idea to ask a few of the children for examples of words with more than one syllable.

'Jane, do you know any multi-syllable words?'

After some thought Jane proudly replies, 'Monday.'

'Great Jane. That has two syllables, Mon…day. Does anyone know another word?'

'I do! I do!' replies Johnny.

Knowing Johnny's more mature sense of humour she picks Mike instead. 'OK Mike, what is your word.'

'Saturday,' says Mike.

'Great, that has three syllables.'

Not wanting to be outdone, Johnny says, 'I know a four-syllable word. Pick me! Pick me!'

Not thinking he can do any harm with a word that large the teacher reluctantly says, 'OK. Johnny what is your four-syllable word?'

Johnny proudly says, 'Mas…tur…ba…tion.'

Shocked, the teacher, trying to retain her composure says, 'Wow, Johnny. Four syllables! That certainly is a mouthful.'

'No Ma'am, you're thinking of "blowjob", and that's only two syllables.'

Mikey and Jane are only ten years old, but they just know that they are in love. One day they decide that they want to get married, so Mikey goes to Jane's father to ask him for her hand.

Mikey bravely walks up to him and says, 'Mr Smith, Jane and I are in love and I want to ask you for her hand in marriage.'

Thinking that this is the cutest thing, Mr Smith replies, 'Well Mikey, you are only ten. Where will you two live?'

Without even taking a moment to think about it, Mikey replies, 'In Jane's room. It's bigger than mine and we can both fit there nicely. '

Still thinking this is just adorable, Mr Smith says with a huge grin, 'OK then how will you live? You're not old enough to get a job. You'll need to support Jane.'

Again, Mikey instantly replies. 'Our allowance. Jane makes $5 a week and I make $10 a week. That's about $60 a month, and that'll do us just fine.'

By this time Mr Smith is a little shocked that Mikey has put so much thought into this. So, he thinks for a moment, trying to come up with something that Mikey won't have an answer for.

After a second, Mr Smith says, 'Well Mikey, it seems like you have got everything worked out. I just have one more question for you. What will you do if the two of you should have little ones of your own?'

Mikey just shrugs his shoulders and says, 'Well, we've been lucky so far.'

A little girl is out shopping with her grandmother when they come across a couple of dogs mating on the sidewalk.

'What are they doing, Grandma?' asks the little girl.

The grandmother is embarrassed, so she says, 'The dog on top has hurt his paw, and the one underneath is carrying him to the doctor.'

'They're just like people, aren't they Grandma?'

'How do you mean?' asks the grandmother.

'Offer someone a helping hand,' says the little girl, 'and they screw you every time!'

A boy wakes up in the middle of the night and goes to the bathroom. On the way back to bed, he passes his parents room. When he looks in, he notices the covers bouncing.

He calls to his dad, 'Hey Dad, what are you doing?'

Dad answers, 'Playing cards.'

The boy asks, 'Who's your partner?'

Dad answers, 'Your mum.'

The boy then passes by his older sister's room. Again, he notices the covers bouncing.

He calls to his sister, 'Hey Sis, what are you doing?'

The sister answers, 'Playing cards.'

The boy asks, 'Who's your partner?'

She answers, 'My boyfriend.'

A little later, dad gets up and goes to the bathroom. As he passes the boy's room, he notices the covers bouncing.

He calls to his son, 'What are you doing?'

The boy answers, 'Playing cards.'

Dad asks, 'Really? Who's your partner?'

The boy answers, 'You don't need a partner if you have a good hand.'

L ittle Johnny comes home from Catholic school with a black eye.

His father sees it and says, 'Johnny, how many times do I have to tell you not to fight with the other boys?'

'But Dad, it wasn't my fault. We were all in church saying our prayers. We all stood up and my teacher in front of me had her dress in the crack of her bum. I reached over and pulled it out. That's when she hit me.'

'Johnny,' the father says, 'you don't do those kinds of things to women.'

Sure enough, the very next day Johnny comes home with the other eye black and blue. Johnny's father says, 'Johnny, I thought we had a talk.'

'But Dad,' Johnny says, 'It wasn't my fault. There we were in church saying our prayers. We all stood up and my teacher in front of us had her dress in the crack of her bum. Then Louie, who was sitting next to me, saw it and he reached over and pulled it out. Now I know she doesn't like this, so I pushed it back in.'

Little Johnny, on a particularly reckless day, is playing in the backyard. Soon, some honeybees start swirling around, annoying little Johnny. He stomps on them in his temper.

His father catches him trampling the honeybees and, after a brief moment of thought, he says, 'That's it! No honey for you for one month!'

Later that afternoon, Johnny sees some butterflies, and soon starts catching them and crushing them under his feet.

His father again catches him and, after a brief moment of thought, says, 'No butter for you for one month!'

Early that evening, Johnny's mother is cooking dinner, and gets jumpy when cockroaches start scurrying around the kitchen floor. She begins stomping on them one by one until all the cockroaches are dead. Johnny's mother looks up to find Johnny and his father watching her.

Johnny says, 'Are you going to tell her, Daddy, or should I?'

Two little boys go into a grocery store. One is nine, one is four.

The nine-year-old grabs a box of tampons from the shelf and carries it to the register.

The cashier asks, 'Oh, these must be for your mum, huh?'

The nine-year-old replies, 'Nope, not for my mum.'

Without thinking, the cashier responds, 'Well, they must be for your sister then?'

The nine-year-old quips, 'Nope, not for my sister either.'

The cashier has now become curious. 'Oh. Not for your mum and not for your sister, who are they for?'

The nine-year-old says, 'They're for my four-year-old little brother.'

The cashier is surprised. 'Your four-year-old little brother?'

The nine-year-old explains, 'Well yeah, they say on TV if you wear one of these you can swim or ride a bike and my little brother can't do either of them!'

The first grade class gathered around the teacher for a game of 'Guess the Animal'. The first picture the teacher held up was of a cat.

'OK, boys and girls,' she said brightly, 'can anyone tell me what this is?'

'I know, I know, it's a cat!' yelled a little boy.

'Very good, Eddie. Now, who knows what this animal is called?'

'That's a dog!' piped up the same little boy.

'Right, again. And what about this animal?' She asked, holding up a picture of a deer.

Silence fell over the class. After a minute or two, the teacher said, 'I'll give you a hint, children. It's something you're mother calls your father.'

'I know, I know,' screamed Eddie. 'It's a horny bastard!'

SALLY: Mummy why can't I go swimming in the sea?
MUM: Because there are sharks in the sea.
SALLY: But mummy, daddy is swimming in the sea.
MUM: That's different. He's insured.

A few months after his parents' divorce, little Johnny passes by his mum's bedroom and sees her rubbing her body and moaning, 'I need a man, I need a man!'

Over the next couple of months, he sees her doing this several times. One day, he comes home from school and hears her moaning. When he peeks into her bedroom, he sees a man on top of her.

Little Johnny runs into his room, takes off his clothes, throws himself on his bed, starts stroking himself and moans, 'Ohh, I need a bike! I need a bike!'

WOMAN: Your son is terribly spoiled.
MOTHER: How dare you. He's not spoiled at all.
WOMAN: Yes he is. He just got hit by a bus.

Mummy, mummy, why can't we give Grandma a proper burial?

Shut up and keep flushing.

Mummy, mummy, daddy's on fire.

Hurry up and get the marshmallows.

Mummy, mummy, my head hurts.

Shut up and get away from the dart board.

Mummy, mummy, why can't we buy a garbage disposal unit?

Shut up and keep chewing.

Mummy, mummy, dad's going out.

Shut up and throw some more petrol on him.

Mummy, mummy, daddy's hammering on the roof again.

Shut up and drive a bit faster.

While in the playground with his friend, Alex notices that Jimmy is wearing a brand-new, shiny watch.

'Did you get that for your birthday?' asks Alex.

'Nope,' replies Jimmy.

'Well, did you get it for Christmas then?'

Again Jimmy says, 'Nope.'

'You didn't steal it, did you?' asks Alex.

'No,' says Jimmy. 'I went into mum and dad's bedroom the other night when they were "doing the nasty". Dad gave me his watch to get rid of me.'

Alex is extremely impressed with this idea, and extremely jealous of Jimmy's new watch. He vows to get one for himself. That night, he waits outside his parents' bedroom until he hears the unmistakable noises of lovemaking. Just then, he swings the door wide open and boldly strides into the bedroom.

His father, caught in mid-stroke, turns and says angrily, 'What do you want now?'

'I wanna watch,' Alex replies.

Without missing a stroke, his father says, 'Fine. Stand in the corner and watch, but keep quiet.'

THAT'S DISGUSTING!

A woman walks into a tattoo parlour and says she wants a tattoo of a turkey on her right inner thigh, just below her bikini area.

'And write "Happy Thanksgiving" under the turkey,' she adds.

So the tattoo artist does as he is told.

Next, the woman instructs him to put a Santa tattoo with 'Merry Christmas' on her left inner thigh.

So the guy does it and the woman is satisfied.

As she is getting dressed to leave, the tattoo artist asks, 'If you don't mind me asking, why did you want such unusual tattoos on your thighs?'

'I'm sick of my husband always complaining that there's nothing good to eat between Thanksgiving and Christmas!'

The Smiths have no children and decide to use a proxy father to start their family. On the day the proxy father is to arrive, Mr Smith kisses his wife and says, 'I'm off. The man should be here soon.'

Half an hour later, just by chance, a door-to-door baby photographer rings the doorbell, hoping to make a sale.

'Good morning madam. You don't know me but I've come to –'

'Oh, no need to explain. I've been expecting you,' Mrs Smith cuts in.

'Really?' the photographer asks. 'Well, good! I've made a specialty of babies.'

'That's what my husband and I had hoped. Please come in and have a seat. Just where do we start?' asks Mrs Smith, blushing.

'Leave everything to me. I usually try two in the bathtub, one on the couch and perhaps a couple on the bed. Sometimes the living room floor is fun too; you can really spread out.'

'Bathtub, living room floor? No wonder it didn't work for Harry and me.'

'Well madam, none of us can guarantee a good one every time. But if we try several different positions and I shoot from six or seven angles, I'm sure you'll be pleased with the results.'

'I hope we can get this over with quickly,' gasps Mrs Smith.

'Madam, in my line of work, a man must take his time. I'd love to be in and out in five minutes, but you'd be disappointed with that, I'm sure.'

'Don't I know it!' Mrs Smith exclaims.

The photographer opens his briefcase and pulls out a portfolio of his baby pictures. 'This was done on the top of a bus in the middle of London.'

'Oh my god!' Mrs Smith exclaims, tugging at her handkerchief.

'And these twins turned out exceptionally well, when you consider their mother was so difficult to work with.' The photographer hands Mrs Smith the picture.

'She was difficult?' asks Mrs Smith.

'Yes, I'm afraid so. I finally had to take her to Hyde Park to get the job done right. People were crowding around four and five deep, pushing to get a good look.'

'Four and five deep?' asks Mrs Smith, eyes wide in amazement.

'Yes,' the photographer says. 'And for more than three hours too. The mother was constantly squealing and yelling. I could hardly concentrate. Then darkness approached and I began to rush my shots. Finally, when the squirrels began nibbling on my equipment I just packed it all in.'

Mrs Smith leans forward. 'You mean they actually chewed on your, er…um…ah…equipment?'

'That's right. Well madam, if you're ready, I'll set up my tripod so that we can get to work.'

'Tripod?' Mrs Smith looks extremely worried now.

'Oh yes, I have to use a tripod to rest my Canon on. It's much too big for me to hold while I'm getting ready for action.

Madam? Madam?…Good Lord, she's fainted!'

A construction worker on the third floor of a building needs a handsaw. He sees one of the labourers on the first floor and yells down to him, but the man indicates that he cannot hear. So, the guy on the third floor tries to use signals. He points to his eye meaning 'I' then at his knee meaning 'need' then he moves his hand back and forth meaning 'handsaw'.

The man on the first floor nods, then drops his pants and begins to masturbate. The man on the third floor freaks out and runs down to the first floor yelling, 'What the hell is wrong with you! Are you stupid or something? I was saying that I needed a handsaw!'

The labourer looks at the construction worker and says, 'I knew that, I was just trying to tell you that I was coming.'

One day Bill complains to his friend, 'My elbow really hurts, I guess I should see a doctor.'

His friend offers, 'Don't do that. There's a computer at the chemist that can diagnose anything quicker and cheaper than a doctor. Simply put in a sample of your urine and the computer will diagnose your problem and tell you what you can do about it. It only costs $10.'

Bill reckons he has nothing to lose, so he fills a jar with a urine sample and goes to the chemist. Finding the computer, he pours in the sample and deposits the $10. The computer starts making some noise and various lights start flashing. After a brief pause out pops a small slip of paper on which is printed: 'You have tennis elbow. Soak your arm in warm water. Avoid heavy lifting. It will be better in two weeks.'

Late that evening, while thinking how amazing this new technology is and how it will change medical science forever, Bill begins to wonder if this machine can be fooled. He decides to give it a try. He mixes together some tap water, a stool sample from his dog and urine samples from his wife and daughter. To top it off, he masturbates into the concoction.

He goes back to the chemist, locates the machine, pours in the sample and deposits the $10. The computer again makes the noise and prints out the following message: 'Your tap water is too hard. Get a water softener. Your dog has worms. Get him vitamins. Your daughter is using cocaine. Put her in a rehabilitation clinic. Your wife is pregnant with twin girls. They aren't yours. Get a lawyer. And if you don't stop jerking off, your tennis elbow will never get better.'

A professor is sent to live with a primitive tribe. He spends years with them, teaching them reading, writing, maths and science. One day the wife of the tribe's chief gives birth to a white child.

The members of the tribe are shocked, and the chief pulls the professor aside and says, 'Look here! You're the only white man we've ever seen and this woman gave birth to a white child. It doesn't take a genius to work out what happened!'

The professor thinks quickly, 'No, Chief. You're mistaken. What you have here is a natural occurrence…what we in the civilised world call an albino! Look at that field over there. All of the sheep are white except for one black one. Nature does this on occasion.'

The chief is silent for a moment, then says, 'Tell you what. You don't say anything more about the sheep and I won't say anything more about the baby.'

After a few years of married life, a guy finds that he is unable to perform anymore. He goes to his doctor, and his doctor tries a few things but nothing works.

Finally the doctor says to him, 'This is all in your mind,' and refers him to a psychiatrist.

After a few visits to the shrink, the shrink confesses, 'I am at a loss as to how you can possibly be cured.'

Finally the psychiatrist refers him to a witch doctor.

The witch doctor says, 'I can cure this,' and throws some powder on a flame. There is a flash with billowing blue smoke.

The witch doctor says, 'This is powerful healing but you can only use it once a year! All you have to do is say "one, two, three" and it shall rise for as long as you wish!'

The guy then asks the witch doctor, 'What happens when it's over?'

The witch doctor says, 'All you or your partner has to say is "one, two, three, four" and it will go down. But be warned it will not work again for a year.'

The guy goes home and that night he is ready to surprise his wife with the good news.

So he is lying in bed with her and says, 'One, two, three.'

Suddenly he gets an erection.

His wife turns over and says, 'What did you say "one, two, three" for?'

A little old lady goes into a bank one day, carrying a bag of money. She asks to speak with the bank manager to open an account. The staff usher her into the manager's office and the manager asks how much she wants to deposit.

She replies, '$165 000!' and dumps the cash on his desk. The manager is curious as to how she came by all this cash, so he asks her, 'Ma'am, where did you get this money?'

The old lady replies, 'I make bets.'

The manager then asks, 'Bets? What kind of bets?'

The old woman says, 'Well, for example, I'll bet you $25 000 that your balls are square.'

'Ha!' laughs the manager, 'That's a stupid bet. You can never win that kind of bet!'

The old lady challenges, 'So, would you like to take my bet?'

'Sure,' says the manager, 'I'll bet $25 000 that my balls are not square!'

The old lady says, 'OK, but since there is a lot of money involved, may I bring my lawyer with me tomorrow at 10 a.m. as a witness?'

'Sure!' replies the confident manager.

That night, he is very nervous about the bet and often checks his balls in the mirror. The next morning, at precisely 10 a.m., the little old lady appears with her lawyer at the manager's office. She introduces the lawyer to the manager and repeats the bet, '$25 000 says the manager's balls are square'.

The manager agrees with the bet again and the old lady asks him to drop his pants so they can all see. The manager complies. The little old lady peers closely at his balls and then asks if she can feel them.

'Well, OK,' says the manager, 'I suppose $25 000 is a lot of money, so you should be absolutely sure.'

Just then, he notices that the lawyer is quietly banging his head against the wall. The manager says, 'What's wrong with your lawyer?'

She replies, 'Nothing, except I bet him $100 000 that at 10 a.m. today, I'd have the bank manager's balls in my hand!'

A representative for a condom company is on her way to an international condom convention. While rushing through the airport, she drops the briefcase carrying her samples, scattering condoms across the floor. She notices a passer-by looking at her as she tries to get the condoms back into her briefcase.

'It's OK,' she says. 'I'm going to a convention.'

A beautiful woman loves growing tomatoes, but can't seem to get her tomatoes to turn red. One day while taking a stroll she comes upon a male neighbour who has the most beautiful garden full of huge red tomatoes.

The woman asks the man, 'What do you do to get your tomatoes so red?'

The man responds, 'Well, twice a day I stand in front of my tomato garden and expose myself, and my tomatoes turn red from blushing so much.'

Well, the woman is so impressed, she decides to try doing the same thing to her tomato garden to see if it works. So twice a day for two weeks she exposes herself to her garden hoping for the best.

One day the man is passing by and asks the woman, 'By the way, how did you make out? Did your tomatoes turn red?'

'No' she replies, 'but my cucumbers are enormous.'

Little Red Riding Hood is skipping down the road when she sees the Big Bad Wolf crouched down behind a log.

'My, what big eyes you have, Mr Wolf,' says Little Red Riding Hood.

The wolf jumps up and runs away. Further down the road Little Red Riding Hood sees the wolf again. This time he is crouched behind a tree stump.

'My, what big ears you have Mr Wolf,' says Little Red Riding Hood.

Again the wolf jumps up and runs away. Further down the track Little Red Riding Hood sees the wolf again, this time crouched down behind a road sign.

'My, what big teeth you have Mr Wolf,' taunts Little Red Riding Hood.

With that the Big Bad Wolf jumps up and screams, 'Will you piss off! I'm trying to take a shit.'

A high court judge is at a bar in a high-class hotel where he is a regular visitor. He drinks into the small hours of the morning. On leaving the bar he vomits down the front of his suit then staggers to his parked car, which he manages to start and drives home in a most dangerous fashion. When he arrives at his mansion in a suburb, he falls out of the car, and staggers to the door, which his wife has opened. On seeing his state she asks what happened. Despite his condition, he thinks quickly.

'I had a few civil drinks in the Shelburne hotel, and when I came out a drunk got sick all over me. But the police caught him and he's up in front of me in the morning. I'll give the swine six months in jail,' he replies.

His wife then sends him to the shower and then bed, while she makes him some food and a hot drink. Having put his soiled clothes in the wash she returns to the bedroom with his food.

'How long did you say you would give the drunk in jail?' she asks.

'Six months,' he replies.

'Well you better make it twelve because he shat in your pants as well.'

A white guy in a bar goes to the toilet. While he's standing there, a black guy comes in, stands beside him and whips out his massive dong. The white guy asks him how he got it. The black guy tells him, 'Every night I tie a piece of cord round the end and pull it tight for five minutes.'

The white guy thanks him and leaves. The two meet up in the same toilets six months later.

'How are you doin' with the dick,' says the black guy.

'Excellent,' says the white guy, 'look it's nearly all black.'

A mother and father take their young son to the circus. When the elephants appear, the son is intrigued by them. He turns to his mother and says, 'Mum, what's that hanging between the elephant's legs?'

The mother is very embarrassed, and says, 'Oh, it's nothing son.'

So the son turns to his father and asks the same question.

The father replies, 'It's the elephant's penis, son.'

So the son says, 'Why did mum say it was nothing?'

The father draws himself up, and says proudly, 'Because I've spoiled that woman, son.'

A man and his young son are in the chemist when the son comes across the condoms and asks his father what they are. The dad replies, 'Well son, those are condoms and they're for protection when you're having sex.'

The son then picks up one of the packs and asks why it has three condoms in it.

The dad replies, 'Those are for high-school boys. One for Friday, one for Saturday, and one for Sunday.'

The son then picks up one with six condoms and asks, 'Why six?' The dad replies, 'Well son, those are for uni students. Two for Friday, two for Saturday and two for Sunday.'

The son then notices the twelve-pack of condoms and asks the same question. The dad replies, 'Son, those are for married men. One for January, one for February, one for March…'

Two lovers are really into spiritualism and reincarnation. They vow that if either dies, the one remaining will try to contact the partner in the other world exactly thirty days after the death. Unfortunately, a few weeks later, the young man dies in a car crash. True to her word, his sweetheart tries to contact him in the spirit world exactly thirty days later.

At the séance, she calls out, 'John, John, this is Martha. Do you hear me?'

A ghostly voice answers her, 'Yes Martha, this is John. I can hear you.'

Martha tearfully asks, 'Oh John, what is it like where you are?'

'It's great. There are azure skies, a soft breeze, sunshine most of the time, the grass is green and the cows have beautiful eyes.'

'What do you do all day?' asks Martha.

'Well, Martha, we get up before sunrise, eat a good breakfast, and then there's nothing but making love until noon. After lunch, we nap until two and then make love again until about five. After dinner, we go at it again until we fall asleep about 11 p.m.'

Martha is somewhat taken aback. 'Is that what heaven really is like?'

'Heaven? I'm not in heaven, Martha.'

'Well, then, where are you?'

'I'm a bull on a stud farm.'

Bill Bodgy is a travelling toy salesman who is going through a period of low sales. He arrives one morning at the door of a large mansion, and is met by a nine-year-old boy.

He enquires if either of the boy's parents are home, and receives a negative reply.

He tells the boy that he is selling the latest thing in trail bikes, and will come back later in order to speak to the boy's parents. The boy tells him not to bother, since he is too advanced for that sort of thing.

The salesman tries to push his product, and then foolishly agrees that if he can do everything the boy can do, the boy will ask for a bike for Christmas. If not, then Bill must give him a bike. First of all, the boy jumps onto the roof of a nearby shed, balances along the ridge, and jumps off with a somersault. Thanking his lucky stars he has kept fit, Bill copies him. Next the boy does five handstands on the lawn, with the same response from Bill. The boy then takes Bill into the house, and into a rear bedroom, in which a stunning twenty-five-year-old girl is lying in bed.

'My cousin Jackie,' explains the boy. 'She's a flight attendant with Qantas, and has just come off an international flight and taken a couple of sleeping pills. Nothing will wake her. Is this deal still on?'

Somewhat apprehensive, but desperate for a sale, Bill agrees. The boy pulls down the bedclothes to reveal a skimpy negligee and undies. He then replaces the bedclothes, and invites Bill to copy his actions. Sweat breaking from his brow, Bill does as invited. The boy then pulls down the bedclothes a second time, and slides the negligee up to reveal the most immaculate pair of tits. Bill does the same, now trembling. The boy then slides down the undies half of the nightie, to reveal all. Shaking like a leaf, Bill follows suit.

The boy then takes out his dick, folds it in half, and announces, 'I'll have a red one with racing handles.'

A pianist is hired to play background music for a movie. When it is completed he asks when and where he can see the film. The producer sheepishly confesses that it is actually a porno film and it is due out in a month. A month later, the musician goes to a porno theatre to see it. With his collar up and dark glasses on, he takes a seat in the back row, next to a couple who also seem to be in disguise.

The movie is even raunchier than he had feared, featuring group sex, S&M and even a dog. After a while, the embarrassed pianist turns to the couple and says, 'I'm only here to listen to the music.'

'Yeah?' replies the man. 'We're only here to see our dog.'

P ingi the penguin is a long-haul truck driver. One day, while driving across a desert, his truck starts to play up. Spotting a garage in the distance, he coaxes his vehicle to it, and asks the mechanic to have a look at it.

Finding the heat of the sun unbearable, as penguins are wont to do, Pingi retreats into the cafe and has a couple of cooling drinks. Still hot, he then has some ice-cream, but as penguins are not built to handle ice-cream (flippers being most unsuitable), most of the ice-cream ends up all over him.

Covered with ice-cream, he wanders back to where the mechanic is finishing up.

'How are things going?' asks Pingi.

'It looks like you've blown a seal,' says the mechanic.

'Oh no,' replies Pingi, 'it's ice-cream.'

A husband suspects his wife is having an affair. He needs to go on a business trip for several days, so he decides to set a trap for her. He puts a bowl of milk under the bed. From the bed springs, he suspends a spoon. He has it calibrated so that her weight on the bed will not drop the spoon into the milk. But, if there is any more weight than that, the spoon will drop into the milk and he will detect it upon his return home.

He comes home several days later. The first thing he does is reach under the bed and retrieve the bowl. It's full of butter.

Andy bumps into his friend Fred, who looks very upset.

'What's wrong?' Andy asks.

'My brother just told me that there's a sperm bank in his neighbourhood that pays $50 for a donation.'

'And?'

'Don't you realise?' Fred cries. 'I've let a fortune slip through my fingers!'

Two women are at their local shopping mall, when one happens to see her husband emerging from a florist shop carrying a large bunch of roses.

'Oh no,' she says. 'Looks like I'll have to spread the legs tonight.'

'Why?' asks the other. 'Don't you own a vase?'

A guy buys a second-hand Harley Davidson, which is almost in mint condition. Before riding off, he asks the owner how he managed to keep it in such good shape.

'Well,' says the owner, 'it's pretty simple. Just make sure that if the bike is outside and it's going to rain, rub Vaseline on the chrome. It protects it from the rain.'

The next night, the guy goes over to his girlfriend's house for dinner. It's the first time he's been there and she meets him on the doorstep.

'Honey,' she says, 'I gotta tell you something about my parents before you go in. When we eat dinner, we don't talk. In fact, the person who says anything during dinner has to do the dishes.'

'No problem,' he says. And in they go.

The boyfriend is astounded. Right smack in the middle of the living room is a huge stack of dirty dishes. In the family room, another huge stack of dishes. Piled up the stairs, dirty dishes. In fact, everywhere he looks, dirty dishes. They sit down to dinner and, sure enough, no-one says a word. As dinner progresses, the boyfriend decides to take advantage of the situation. So he leans over and kisses his girlfriend. No-one says a word. So he decides to reach over and fondle her breasts. He looks at her parents, but still they keep quiet. So he stands up, grabs his girlfriend, strips her naked, and they make love right on the dinner table. Still, no-one says a word.

'Her mum's kinda cute,' he thinks. So he grabs his girlfriend's mum and has his way with her right there on the dinner table.

Again, total silence. Then, a few raindrops hit the window and the boyfriend realises it's starting to rain. He thinks he'd better take care of the motorcycle, so he pulls the Vaseline from his pocket.

Suddenly the father stands up and shouts, 'All right, all right! I'll do the damn dishes.'

A convicted murderer escapes from prison after spending twenty-five years inside. While on the run, he breaks into a house and ties up a young couple who have been sleeping in the bedroom. He ties the man to a chair on one side of the room and ties the woman to the bed. He gets on the bed right over the woman, and appears to be kissing her neck.

Suddenly he gets up and leaves the room, though not the house.

As soon as possible the husband makes his way across the room to his bride, his chair in tow, and whispers, 'Honey, this guy hasn't seen a woman in years. I saw him kissing your neck. Just cooperate and do anything he wants. If he wants to have sex with you, just go along with it and pretend you like it. Whatever you do don't fight him or make him mad. Our lives depend on it! Be strong and I love you.'

After spitting out the gag in her mouth, the half-naked wife says, "Darling, I'm so relieved you feel that way. You're right, he hasn't seen a woman in years, but he wasn't kissing my neck. He was whispering in my ear. He said he thinks you're really cute and asked if we kept the Vaseline in the bathroom. Be strong and I love you, too.'

A middle-aged man and woman meet, fall in love and decide to get married. On their wedding night they settle into the bridal suite at their hotel and the bride says to her new groom, 'Please promise to be gentle…I am still a virgin.'

The startled groom asks, 'How can that be? You've been married three times before.'

The bride responds, 'Well you see it was this way: My first husband was a psychiatrist and all he ever wanted to do was talk about it. My second husband was a gynaecologist and all he ever wanted to do was look at it. My third husband was a stamp collector and all he ever wanted to do was…God I miss him.'

A woman is in the kitchen making dinner when her daughter walks in.

'Mum, where do babies come from?'

After a moment's hesitation the mother says, 'Well, the mummy and daddy fall in love and get married. One night they go to their room and they kiss each other, hug each other and have sex.'

The daughter looks puzzled. The mother goes on, 'That means the daddy puts his penis in the mummy's vagina. That's how you get babies.'

The daughter replies, 'OK, but the other night when I came into your room daddy's penis was in your mouth. What do you get when you do that?'

'Jewellery, dear.'

A couple are having a quickie in the back of a car in a dark lane.

The man says to the woman, 'This is fantastic, but why are your ankles banging against my ears?'

'I've still got my tights on.'

Three sisters decide to get married on the same day to save their parents the expense of separate weddings. As a further step to reduce the price tag, the three sisters resolve to spend their honeymoon night at home. Later that night, their mother can't sleep, so she goes to the kitchen for a cup of tea. On her way, she tiptoes by her oldest daughter's bedroom and hears her screaming.

The mother thinks to herself, 'That's normal, especially on her wedding night.'

She sneaks by her second-oldest daughter's room and hears her laughing.

'That's normal too,' she says, smiling to herself.

Finally, she slips by her youngest daughter's room where she doesn't hear a peep, but she thinks nothing of it. The next morning in the kitchen, after the husbands have gone out, the woman asks her eldest daughter about last night's noises.

'Well Mum,' she replies, 'you always said if it hurt I should scream.'

'You're absolutely right sweetheart,' the mother assures her, and turns to her middle daughter.

'Now why were you laughing?' she asks.

'You always said if it tickled, I could laugh,' she answers.

'True enough, honey.' The mother smiles, remembering her newlywed days.

'Now it's your turn, baby,' she says, turning to her youngest daughter. 'Why was it so quiet in your room last night?'

'Mum, don't you remember? You always told me never to talk with my mouth full.'

A couple are going through some tough times, so they agree that the woman will walk the streets for a night and see if she can make a bit of money. The guy drops her off on a corner in a rough area of town and drives off. The next morning he picks her up and finds her with her hair a mess, make-up smudged and obviously needing a lot of rest.

She climbs in the car and excitedly says, 'Look honey, I made $40.50.'

'Which of the buggers gave you fifty cents?' he asks.

'All of them!' she says.

A hippie gets onto a bus and sits next to a nun in the front seat. The hippie looks over and asks the nun if she will have sex with him. The nun, surprised by the question, politely declines and gets off at the next stop.

When the bus starts on its way the driver says to the hippie, 'I can tell you how you can get that nun to have sex with you.'

The hippie says that he'd love to know, so the bus driver tells him that every Tuesday evening at midnight the nun goes to the cemetery and prays to God. 'If you went dressed in a robe and glow in the dark paint mask she would think you are God and you could command her to have sex with you.'

The hippie decides this is a great idea, so the next Tuesday he goes to the cemetery and waits for the nun to show up. At midnight, sure enough, the nun shows up and begins praying.

The hippie jumps out from hiding and says, 'I am God! I have heard your prayers and I will answer them, but…first you must have sex with me.'

The nun agrees but asks for anal sex so she might keep her virginity, because she is married to the church. The hippie agrees to this and has his way with the nun.

After the hippie finishes he stands up and rips off the mask and shouts, 'Ha! Ha! Ha! I'm the hippie!'

Then the nun jumps up and shouts, 'Ha! Ha! Ha! I'm the bus driver!'

A man is at home watching TV and eating peanuts. He tosses a peanut in the air, and then catches it in his mouth. In the middle of catching a peanut, his wife asks him a question. As he turns to answer her, the peanut falls into the man's ear. He tries to dig the peanut out, but it only goes further into his ear. His wife tries to help but to no avail.

They decide to go to the hospital, but as they are about to leave, their daughter comes home with her date.

After being informed of the problem, their daughter's date says he can get the peanut out.

The young man sits the father down, shoves two fingers up his nose and tells him to blow hard. When the father blows, the peanut flies out.

The mother and daughter are impressed. The young man insists that it was nothing. He goes home and the daughter goes to bed. Once they are gone, the mother turns to the father.

'He's so smart! I wonder what he's going to be when he grows up!'

'From the smell of his fingers, our son-in-law.'

Three prostitutes are living together: a mother, a daughter and a grandmother. One night the daughter comes home looking very down.

'How did you do tonight, dear?' asks her mother.

'Not too good,' replies the daughter, 'I only got $20 for a blow job.'

'Wow!' says the mother. 'In my day, we were glad to get $5 for a blow job!'

'Good God!' says the grandmother. 'In my day, we were glad just to get something warm in our stomachs!'

A woman is sitting on a beach, attempting to strike up a conversation with the attractive gentleman reading on the blanket beside hers.

'Hello, Sir,' she says. 'Do you like movies?'

'Yes, I do,' he responds, then returns to his book.

She persists, 'Do you like gardening?'

The man again looks up from his book. 'Yes, I do,' he says politely before returning to his reading.

Undaunted, she asks, 'Do you like pussycats?'

With that, the man drops his book and pounces on her, ravishing her as she's never been ravished before.

As the cloud of sand begins to settle, the woman drags herself to a sitting position and pants, 'How did you know that was what I wanted?'

The man thinks for a moment and replies, 'How did you know my name was Katz?'

Jim phones his office in the morning and says to his boss, 'Boss, I'm not coming in today, I'm sick.'

His boss says, 'Exactly how sick are ya?'

Jim replies, 'Well, I'm in bed with my sister!'

A king and a queen rule a large kingdom. The king is short in vital parts and the queen has to seek solace with every Tom, Dick and Harry. After some time, the king grows suspicious of the queen's escapades and wants to punish the subjects willing to risk their lives for a fling with her.

He seeks the services of his court magician to help identify the culprits. The magician builds an invisible contraption that is attached to the queen's waist. The mechanism is simple, it slices any elongated object that ventures anywhere within an inch of the queen's waist.

Having set his trap the king sets off on a hunting trip and returns to his palace, after spending a sleepless week, burning with curiosity. Immediately after his arrival he summons the queen's private bodyguards to his foyer and dispatches all his attendants. He orders them to undress. All of them have lost their penises! He next summons the palace guards and the result is the same. By mid-afternoon he realises that there is not a single male soul in the vicinity who had not made a valiant attempt only to be left without a penis.

The only man left is his minister and, to his surprise, the king finds him to be the only man who has a penis left.

Pleased with his minister's loyalty, he asks him what punishment would befit all the others. In reply, he receives only a blubbering sound from the minister's mouth.

HAPPY FAMILIES

Two high school sweethearts decided to stay together after high school even though they were going to university on opposite sides of the country. They agreed to be faithful to each other and spend any time they could together.

As time went on, the guy would call the girl and she would never be home. She avoided his emails and wouldn't get back to him for weeks.

Finally, she confessed that she had started seeing someone else. He didn't take this well and started to call her nonstop, trying his best to get her back.

The girl got annoyed so she took a photo of herself with her new boyfriend's penis in her mouth and sent it to the old boyfriend with a note saying, 'I have a new boyfriend, stop calling me.'

The guy was heartbroken but more than that, he was angry.

He wrote on the back of the photo, 'Dear Mum and Dad, having a great time at uni, please send more money!' and mailed the picture to her parents.

A woman in the hospital has just had twins, a boy and a girl. She had a caesarean and is in the recovery room just coming out of the anaesthetic.

The nurse comes into the room and says, 'Your brother has taken the liberty to name the children.'

'Oh no. He probably gave them stupid names.'
'Well, the girl's name is Denise.'
'That's not bad, I like it. What about the boy?'
'The boy's name is De-nephew.'

A woman gets on a bus with her baby. The bus driver says, 'That's the ugliest baby that I've ever seen. Ugh!'
The woman goes to the rear of the bus and sits down, fuming. She says to a man next to her, 'The driver just insulted me!'

'You go right up there and tell him off – go ahead, I'll hold your monkey for you.'

A young woman was taking an afternoon nap. When she woke up, she told her husband, 'I just dreamed that you gave me a pearl necklace for Valentine's day. What do you think it means?'

'You'll find out tonight,' he said.

That evening, the man came home with a small package and gave it to his wife. Delighted, she opened it. It was a book entitled *The Meaning of Dreams*.

Two cannibals are eating their dinner and one cannibal says to the other, 'I don't like my mother-in-law much.'
'Well, just eat your chips then.'

HUSBAND: Shall we try a new position tonight?
WIFE: Sure. You stand by the ironing board and I'll sit on the couch and drink beer and fart.

A newlywed farmer and his wife were visited by her mother, who immediately demanded an inspection of their home. The farmer had tried to be friendly to his new mother-in-law, hoping that theirs would be a non-antagonistic relationship.

All to no avail. She nagged them at every opportunity, demanding changes, offering unwanted advice, and generally making life unbearable for the farmer and his new bride.

During a forced inspection of the barn, the farmer's mule suddenly reared up and kicked the mother-in-law in the head, killing her instantly. It was a shock to all, no matter what were their feelings towards her demanding ways.

At the funeral service a few days later, the farmer stood near the casket and greeted folks as they walked by. The pastor noticed that whenever a woman whispered something to the farmer, he would nod his head yes and say something. Whenever a man walked by and whispered to the farmer, however, he would shake his head no, and mumble a reply.

Very curious about this bizarre behaviour, the pastor asked the farmer what was going on.

The farmer replied, 'The women say, "What a terrible tragedy" and I nod my head and say "Yes, it was". The men ask, "Can I borrow that mule?" and I shake my head and say, "I can't lend it to you. It's all booked up for a year"…'

At school, Little Johnny is told by a classmate that most adults are hiding at least one dark secret, and that this makes it very easy to blackmail them by saying, 'I know the whole truth.'

Little Johnny decides to try it out. He goes home, and is greeted by his mother.

He says, 'I know the whole truth.'

His mother quickly hands him $20 and says, 'Just don't tell your father.'

Quite pleased, the boy waits for his father to get home from work, and greets him with, 'I know the whole truth.'

The father promptly hands him $40 and says, 'Please don't say a word to your mother.'

Very pleased, the boy is on his way to school the next day when he sees the mailman at his front door. The boy greets him by saying, 'I know the whole truth.'

The mailman immediately drops the mail, opens his arms, and says, 'Then come give your daddy a great big hug.'

A father and son went fishing one summer day. While they were out in their boat, the boy suddenly became curious about the world around him.

He asked his father, 'Dad, how does this boat float?'

'Don't rightly know son.'

'Dad, how do fish breathe underwater?'

'Don't rightly know son.'

'Dad, why is the sky blue?'

'Don't rightly know son.'

Finally, the boy asked his father, 'Dad, do you mind my asking you all of these questions?'

'Of course not, son. If you don't ask questions, you never learn nothin' at all.'

LITTLE JOHNNY: Mum, when I was on the bus with daddy this morning, he told me to give up my seat to a lady.

MUM: Well, you've done the right thing.

LITTLE JOHNNY: But Mum, I was sitting on daddy's lap.

A little kid gets onto a city bus and sits right behind the driver. He starts yelling, 'If my dad was a bull and my mum a cow I'd be a little bull.'

The driver starts getting mad at the noisy kid, who continues with, 'If my dad was an elephant and my mum an elephant I would be a little elephant.'

The kid goes on with several animals until the bus driver gets angry and yells at the kid, 'What if your dad was gay and your mum was a prostitute?'

The kid smiles and says, 'I would be a bus driver!'

A six-year-old boy called his mother from his friend Charlie's house and confessed he had broken a lamp when he threw a football in their living room.

'But, Mum,' he said, brightening, 'you don't have to worry about buying another one. Charlie's mother said it was irreplaceable.'

Bill and Linda decided that the only way to pull off a Sunday afternoon quickie with their 10-year-old son in the apartment was to send him out on the balcony and order him to report on all the neighbourhood activities.

The boy began his commentary as his parents put their plan into operation.

'There's a car being towed from the parking lot,' he said. 'An ambulance just drove by.'

A few moments passed.

'Looks like the Andersons have company,' he called out.

'Matt's riding a new bike and the Coopers are having sex.'

Mum and dad stop short.

'How do you know that?' the startled father asked.

'Their kid is standing out on the balcony too,' his son replied.

A husband and wife are having passionate sex.

Afterwards, the husband heads to the bathroom. He is halfway down the hall when his eight-year-old son steps into the hallway and is shocked to see his father standing there wearing nothing more than a condom.

'Dad, what are you doing?'

The father, not wanting to explain sex or birth control, makes up a story. 'Well, son, I'm trying to catch a mouse.'

The boy is horrified, 'What are you going to do to the mouse, screw it?'

ANIMALS

A police officer came upon a terrible car crash where two people had been killed. As he looked at the wreckage a little monkey came out of the brush and hopped around the crashed car. The officer looked down at the monkey and said, 'I wish you could talk.'

The monkey looked up at the officer and nodded his head.

'You can understand what I'm saying?' asked the officer.

Again, the monkey nodded.

'Well, did you see what happened?'

The monkey nodded. He pretended to have a can in his hand and turned it up to his mouth.

'They were drinking?' asked the officer.

The monkey nodded.

The monkey then pinched his fingers together and held them to his mouth, sucking deeply.

'They were smoking marijuana too?' asked the officer.

The monkey nodded. He made a sexual sign with his fingers.

'So they were playing around as well!?' asked the astounded officer.

Again, the monkey nodded.

'Now wait, you're saying your owners were drinking, smoking and playing around before they wrecked the car?'

The monkey nodded.

'What were you doing during all this?' asked the officer.

The monkey held up his hands on an imaginary steering wheel.

A local business is looking for office help. They put a sign in the window saying: 'Help Wanted. Must be able to type, must be good with a computer and must be bilingual. We are an Equal Opportunity Employer.'

A short time afterwards, a dog trots up to the window, sees the sign and goes inside. He looks at the receptionist and wags his tail, then walks over to the sign, looks at it and whines.

Getting the idea, the receptionist gets the office manager. The office manager looks at the dog and is surprised, to say the least.

However, the dog looks determined, so he leads him into the office. Inside, the dog jumps up on the chair and stares at the manager.

The manager says, 'I can't hire you. The sign says you have to be able to type.'

The dog jumps down, goes to the typewriter and types out a perfect letter. He takes out the page and trots over to the manager, gives it to him, then jumps back on the chair.

The manager is stunned, but then tells the dog, 'The sign says you have to be good with a computer.'

The dog jumps down again and goes to the computer. He demonstrates his expertise with various programs, produces a sample spreadsheet and database and presents them to the manager.

By this time the manager is totally dumbfounded! He looks at the dog and says, 'I realise that you are a very intelligent dog and have some interesting abilities. However, I still can't give you the job.'

The dog jumps down and goes to the sign and puts his paw on the part about being an Equal Opportunity Employer.

The manager says, 'Yes, but the sign also says that you have to be bilingual.'

The dog looks him straight in the face and says, 'Meow.'

A man with a twenty-five-inch penis goes to his doctor to complain that he is unable to get any women to have sex with him. They all tell him that his penis is too long.

'Doctor,' he asks, in total frustration, 'Is there any way you can shorten it?'

The doctor replies, 'Medically son, there is nothing I can do. But, I do know this witch who may be able to help you.' So the doctor gives him directions to the witch. The man calls upon the witch and relays his story.

'My penis is twenty-five inches long and I can't get any women to have sex with me. Can you help me shorten it?'

The witch stares in amazement, scratches her head and then replies, 'I think I have a solution to your problem. What you have to do is go to this pond deep in the forest. In the pond, you will see a frog sitting on a log who can help solve your dilemma. First you must ask the frog to marry you. Each time the frog declines your proposal, your penis will become five inches shorter.'

The man's face lights up and he dashes off into the forest.

Finding the frog, he says, 'Will you marry me?'

The frog looks at him dejectedly and replies, 'No.'

The man looks down and suddenly his penis is five inches shorter.

'Wow,' he screams out loud. 'This is great. But it's still too long at twenty inches, so I'll ask the frog to marry me again.'

'Frog, will you marry me?' the guy shouts.

The frog rolls its eyes back in its head and screams back, 'No!'

The man feels another twitch in his penis, looks down, and it is another five inches shorter.

The man laughs, 'This is fantastic.' He looks down at his penis again, fifteen inches long, and reflects for a moment. Fifteen inches is still a monster, just a little less would be ideal.

Grinning, he looks across the pond and yells out, 'Frog will you marry me?'

The frog looks back across the pond shaking its head, 'How many damn times do I have to tell you? No, no and for the last time, no!'

A man is driving down the road with twenty penguins in the back seat. The police stop him and say that he can't drive around with the penguins in the car and he should take them to the zoo. The man agrees and drives off. The next day the same man is driving down the road with twenty penguins in the back again.

He is stopped by the same police officer who says, 'Hey! I thought I told you to take those penguins to the zoo.'

The man replies, 'I did. Today I'm taking them to the movies.'

A solicitor from Dublin, while hunting in the west, brought down a fowl, which landed in a farmer's field. As the lawyer climbed over the wall to retrieve the bird, the elderly owner appeared, asking what he was doing.

The litigator replied, 'I shot that bird you see lying there, and now I'm about to pick it up.'

'This is my property you crossing into, and I'm telling you, yer not coming over,' said the old man.

'I'll have you know that I'm one of the best solicitors in all of Ireland, and if you don't let me retrieve my bird, I'll take ye to court for everything y'own!'

'Well now, being as how you're not from around here, you don't know how we settle things like this. You see now, here we use the three-kick method.'

'And what would that be?' asked the lawyer.

'First I kick you three times and then you do the same to me, and back and forth like that till one of us gives up.'

The attorney thought this over, and quickly decided he could easily take on the old codger, and agreed to the local custom.

The old farmer walked slowly over to the lawyer. With his first kick he planted the toe of his heavy boot in the solicitor's groin dropping him to his knees. The second blow nearly wiped the lawyer's nose off his face. The attorney was flat on the ground when the farmer's third kick to the kidney almost finished him.

The lawyer dug deep for his every bit of will, dragged himself standing, and said, 'OK you old bugger, now it's my turn.' The old farmer just smiled and said, 'No, I believe I'll give up now. You can have the bird.'

A little girl asks her mother if she can take the dog for a walk. 'No, honey, because the dog is in heat.'

'What does that mean?' asks the girl.

'Go ask your father.'

The little girl goes to the garage and asks, 'Dad, can I take Susie for a walk around the block? I asked Mum, but she said that Susie was in heat.'

Dad says, 'Bring Susie over here.'

He takes a rag, soaks it with gasoline, and scrubs the dog's rear-end with it.

'OK, you can go now.'

The little girl leaves, and returns a few minutes later without the dog.

Her father asks, 'Where is Susie?'

'She'll be here in a minute. She ran out of gas about halfway down the block and another dog is pushing her home.'

A male whale and a female whale are swimming off the coast of Japan, when they notice a whaling ship. The male whale recognises it as the same ship that had harpooned his father many years earlier.

He says to the female whale, 'Let's both swim under the ship and blow out of our air holes at the same time and it should cause the ship to turn over and sink.'

They try it and sure enough, the ship turns over and quickly sinks.

Soon however, the whales realise that the sailors have jumped overboard and are swimming to the safety of the shore. The male is enraged that they are going to get away and says to the female, 'Let's swim after them and gobble them up before they reach the shore.'

But the female is reluctant to follow him.

'Look,' she says, 'I went along with the blow job, but I absolutely refuse to swallow the seamen.'

A butcher is working when he notices a dog in his shop. He goes to shoo him away when he spots a note in the dog's mouth. The note reads, 'Can I have 12 sausages and a leg of lamb, please?', and wrapped inside the note is a $10 note.

So the butcher takes the money, puts the sausages and lamb in a bag, and places the bag in the dog's mouth. The dog trots happily out of the shop.

Intrigued, the butcher decides to close up shop and follow the dog. It walks down the street and comes to a crossing.

The dog puts down the bag, jumps up and presses the crossing button. Then he waits patiently, bag in mouth, for the lights to change. They do, and he walks across the road, with the butcher following.

The dog comes to a bus stop, and looks at the timetable. Then he sits on one of the seats to wait for the bus. The butcher is in awe.

Along comes a bus. The dog walks to the front of the bus, looks at the number, and goes back to his seat.

Another bus comes. Again the dog checks the number and climbs onto the bus. The butcher, mouth agape, follows him onto the bus.

The bus travels through town and out to the suburbs. Eventually the dog gets up, moves to the front of the bus and, standing on his hind legs, pushes the button to stop the bus.

The dog gets off, meat still in his mouth and the butcher follows. They walk down the road, and the dog approaches a house. He walks up the path, and drops the package of meat on the step.

Then he walks back down the path, takes a big run, and throws himself against the door. He goes back down the path, takes another run, and throws himself against the door again.

There's no answer at the door, so the dog goes to the window and bangs his head against it several times. He sits at the door waiting.

The door swings open. A big bloke looks down at the dog. 'You stupid dog!' he yells.

The butcher is taken aback because, evidently, this dog is not stupid. So he runs up to the bloke and says, 'What the hell are you doing? This dog is a genius. He's so clever, he could be on TV!'

The guy responds, 'Clever? Yeah right. This is the second time this week he's forgotten his key!'

Two guys are out hiking. Suddenly, a bear starts chasing them. They climb a tree, but the bear starts climbing up the tree after them.

The first guy gets his sneakers out of his knapsack and starts putting them on.

'What are you doing?' asks the second guy.

'When the bear gets close to us, I thought we'd jump down and make a run for it.'

'Are you crazy? You can't outrun a bear.'

'I don't have to outrun the bear. I only have to outrun you.'

Twenty puppies were stolen from a pet shop. Police are warning people to look out for anyone selling hot dogs.

A turtle is walking down an alley in New York when he is mugged by a gang of snails. A police detective comes to investigate and asks the turtle if he could explain what happened.

The turtle turns to the detective with a confused look and replies, 'I don't know officer. It all happened so fast...'

An old farmer's rooster was getting along in years so the farmer decided to get a new rooster for his hens. The old rooster saw the young one strutting around and realised that he was being replaced. He decided to do something about it.

He walked up to the new bird and said, 'So you're the new stud in town? Well, I'm not ready for the chopping block yet. To prove it, I challenge you to a race around that hen house over there. We'll run around it 10 times and whoever finishes first gets to have all the hens for himself.'

The young rooster was a proud sort, and he thought he was easily a match for the old guy.

'You're on,' he said, 'and since I'm so great, I'll even give you a head start of half a lap. I'll still win easily!'

So the two roosters went over to the henhouse and all the hens gathered to watch.

The race began and the hens started cheering the old rooster on. After the first lap, the old rooster was still in the lead. After the second lap, the old guy's lead had slipped a little, but he was still hanging in there. Unfortunately, the old rooster's lead continued to slip each time around, and by the fifth lap he was just barely in front of the young fella.

By then the farmer had heard the commotion. He thought there was a fox after his chickens so he ran into the house, got his shotgun and ran into the barnyard.

When he got there, he saw the two roosters running around the henhouse, with the old rooster still slightly in the lead.

He immediately took his shotgun, aimed, fired and blew the young rooster away.

As he walked away he said to himself, 'Damn, that's the third gay rooster I've bought this month.'

Bob was excited about his new rifle and decided to try bear hunting. He travelled up to Alaska, spotted a small brown bear and shot it. Soon after there was a tap on his shoulder, and he turned around to see a big black bear.

The black bear said, 'That was a very bad mistake. That was my cousin. I'm going to give you two choices. Either I maul you to death or we have sex.'

After considering briefly, Bob decided to accept the latter alternative.

So the black bear had his way with Bob.

Even though he felt sore for two weeks, Bob soon recovered and vowed revenge. He headed out on another trip to Alaska where he found the black bear and shot it dead.

Right away, there was another tap on his shoulder. This time a huge grizzly bear stood right next to him.

The grizzly said, 'That was a big mistake, Bob. That was my cousin and you've got two choices. Either I maul you to death or I have sex with you.'

Again, Bob thought it was better to cooperate with the grizzly bear than be mauled to death, so the grizzly had his way with Bob.

Although he survived, it took several months before Bob fully recovered from his run-in with the bear. By then, Bob was completely outraged, so he headed back to Alaska and managed to track down the grizzly bear and shoot it.

He felt the joy of sweet revenge, but then there was a tap on his shoulder. He turned around to find a giant polar bear standing there.

The polar bear looked at him and said, 'Admit it Bob, you don't come here for the hunting, do you?'

There are three dogs all in the pound. The first dog turns to the second dog and asks, 'What are you in for?'

The dog replies, 'Well my master said that if I keep chewing up his newspapers he will put me to sleep. I kept chewing them and today I'm getting put to sleep.'

The other dogs start to comfort him. The second dog turns to the third dog and asks him the same question.

The dog replies, 'Well my master said that if I kept drinking out of the toilet I would get put to sleep. And here I am about to get put to sleep.'

The other dogs start to comfort him too. Then the second and third dog turn to the first dog and ask him the same question.

The dog says, 'When my mistress got out of the shower her towel fell off of her, and when she bent over I just couldn't help myself and started to screw her up the arse.'

The dogs say, 'Oh, we understand why you're getting put to sleep.'

The first dog turns around and says, 'I'm not here to get put to sleep, I'm here to get my nails trimmed.'

GOOD FOR WHAT AILS YOU

A man goes to the doctor complaining that his wife hasn't wanted to have sex with him for six months.

The doctor tells the man to bring his wife in so he can talk to her and determine what the problem is.

The following day, the wife goes to the doctor's office. The doctor asks her why she doesn't want to have sex with her husband.

'Well, for the past six months,' the wife says, 'I've been taking a taxi to work every morning. I don't have any money. The cab driver asks me, "Are you going to pay today, or what?" So, I take an "or what".'

The doctor nods.

'Then, when I get to work,' she continues, 'I'm late, so the boss asks me, "Are we going to write this down in the book, or what?" So, I take an "or what" again.'

The doctor keeps nodding.

'I take a cab home again and the cab driver asks me, "So, are you going to pay this time, or what?" and again, I take an "or what". So you see, doc, by the time I get home I'm all tired out and don't want it anymore.'

'Yes, I see,' replies the doctor. 'So, are we going to tell your husband, or what?'

Adam is walking around the Garden of Eden feeling very lonely, so God asks him, 'What is wrong with you?'

Adam tells God he doesn't have anyone to talk to.

God says, 'And that's a problem? OK, I'll find you some company. This company will cook for you day and night, wash your clothes and keep the garden in order; will bear your children and never ask you to get up in the middle of the night to take care of them; will not nag you, will always be the first to admit being wrong when you've had a disagreement and will always agree with every decision you make. The company will never have a headache, and will freely give you sex, love and compassion whenever needed. But it's going to be expensive Adam. It's going to cost you an arm and a leg.'

'An arm and a leg?' says Adam. 'Wow.'

He thinks for a few seconds, then asks, 'Well, what can I get for just a rib?'

Three guys are having a relaxing day fishing. Out of the blue, they catch a mermaid who begs to be set free, in return for granting each of them a wish.

One of the guys just doesn't believe it, and says, 'OK, if you can really grant wishes, then double my IQ.'

The mermaid says, 'Done!'

Suddenly, the guy starts reciting Shakespeare flawlessly and analysing it with extreme insight.

The second guy is so amazed he says to the mermaid, 'Triple my IQ.'

The mermaid says, 'Done!'

The guy starts to spout out all the mathematical solutions to problems that have been stumping scientists and mathematicians for years.

The last guy is so enthralled with the changes in his friends that he says to the mermaid, 'Quintuple my IQ.'

The mermaid looks at him and says, 'You know, I normally don't try to change people's minds when they make a wish, but I really wish you'd reconsider.'

The guy says, 'Nope, I want you to increase my IQ times five, and if you don't do it, I won't set you free.'

'Please,' says the mermaid. 'You don't know what you're asking. It'll change your entire view on the universe, won't you ask for something else? A million dollars, anything?'

But no matter what the mermaid says, the guy insists on having his IQ increased by five times its usual power.

So the mermaid sighs and says, 'Done.'

And he becomes a woman.

A woman accompanies her husband to the doctor's office. After his check-up, the doctor calls the wife into his office alone. He says, 'Your husband is suffering from a very severe stress disorder. If you don't do the following, he will surely die. Each morning, fix him a healthy breakfast. Be pleasant at all times. For lunch make him a nutritious meal. For dinner prepare an especially nice meal for him. Don't burden him with chores. Don't discuss your problems with him; it will only make his stress worse. No nagging. And most importantly, make love with your husband several times a week. If you can do this for the next 10 months to a year, I think your husband will regain his health completely.'

On the way home, the husband asks his wife, 'What did the doctor say?'

'He said you're going to die,' she replies.

A man brings a very limp dog into the veterinary clinic. As he lays the dog on the table, the doctor pulls out his stethoscope and places the receptor on the dog's chest. After a moment or two, the vet shakes his head sadly and says, 'I'm sorry, but your dog has passed away.'

'What?' screams the man. 'How can you tell? You haven't done any testing on him or anything. I want another opinion.'

With that, the vet turns and leaves the room. In a few moments, he returns with a Labrador Retriever. The Retriever goes right to work, checking the poor dead dog out thoroughly with his nose. After a considerable amount of sniffing, the Retriever sadly shakes his head and says, 'Bark'.

The veterinarian then takes the Labrador out and returns in a few moments with a cat, who also carefully sniffs out the poor dog on the table. As had his predecessors, the cat sadly shakes his head and says, 'Meow'.

He then jumps off the table and runs out of the room. The veterinarian hands the man a bill for $600. The dog's owner goes berserk.

'What, $600! Just to tell me my dog is dead? This is outrageous!'

The vet shakes his head sadly and says, 'If you had taken my word for it, the charge would have been $50, but with the lab work and the cat scan…'

A guy goes to see a doctor and after a series of tests the doctor comes in and says, 'I've got some good news and some bad news.'

'What's the bad news?' asks the patient.

'The bad news is that, unfortunately, you've only got three months to live.'

The patient is shocked, 'Oh my god! Well what's the good news then, doctor?'

The doctor points over to the secretary at the front desk, 'You see that blonde with the big tits, tight arse and legs that go all the way up to heaven?'

The patient says, 'Yes.'

The doctor smiles and replies, 'I'm banging her!'

Mr Smith goes to the doctor's office to collect his wife's test results.

'I'm sorry, Sir,' says the receptionist, 'but there has been a bit of a mix-up and we have a problem. When we sent your wife's sample to the lab, the samples from another Mrs Smith were sent as well and we are now uncertain which one is your wife's. Frankly, that's either bad or terrible.'

'What do you mean?' asks Mr Smith.

'Well, one Mrs Smith has tested positive for Alzheimer's disease and the other for AIDS. We can't tell which your wife's is.'

'That's terrible! Can we take the test over?'

'Normally, yes. But your medical insurance fund won't pay for these expensive tests more than once.'

'Well, what am I supposed to do now?' asks Mr Smith.

'The doctor recommends that you drop your wife off in the middle of town. If she finds her way home, don't sleep with her.'

A proctologist has grown tired of his career and decides to go back to study. After thinking about what he wants to do with the rest of his life, he decides to go to trade school to become a garage mechanic. After struggling through the first course, he takes the final exam. When he gets the results back he is amazed to find he got 200%.

'How in the world did I pass? I thought I was going to flunk this thing,' he says in wonder.

'Well,' replies the instructor, 'I gave you fifty points for getting the engine rebuilt, I gave you fifty points because it ran, and the other 100 points was from doing it all through the muffler.'

A tired doctor is woken by a phone call in the middle of the night.

'Please, you have to come right over,' pleads a distraught young mother. 'My child has swallowed a contraceptive.'

The physician dresses quickly, but before he can get out the door, the phone rings again.

'You don't have to come over after all,' the woman says with a sigh of relief. 'My husband just found another one.'

A man goes to a urologist and tells him that he is having a problem and that he is unable to get his penis erect. After a complete examination, the doctor tells the man that the muscles around the base of his penis are damaged from a prior viral infection and there is nothing he can do for him. However, he knows of an experimental treatment that might be applicable, if the man is willing to take the risk. The treatment consists of implanting muscle tissue from an elephant's trunk into the man's penis.

The man thinks about it for a while. The thought of going through life without ever experiencing sex again is just too much for him to bear. So, with the assurance that there will be no cruelty or adverse effect on the elephant, the man decides to go for it. A few weeks after the operation, he is given the green light to use his newly renovated equipment. As a result, he plans a romantic evening with his girlfriend and takes her to one of the best restaurants in the city.

However, in the middle of dinner, he feels a stirring between his legs that continues to the point of being extremely painful. To release the pressure, he unzips his fly and immediately his penis springs from his pants, goes to the top of the table, grabs a potato, and then returns to his pants.

His girlfriend is stunned at first, but then with a sly smile on her face says, 'That was incredible. Can you do that again?'

With his eyes watering, he replies, 'I think I can, but I'm not sure if I can fit another potato up my arse.'

In a doctor's surgery, Merv sits waiting patiently to see Dr Strangeways. Suddenly, a nun rushes out of his surgery in tears. Somewhat taken aback, Merv goes in next.

'Morning doctor. That nun looked very upset.'

'Yeah, I told her she was pregnant.'

'A nun? Pregnant?'

'Oh, she isn't really. But it sure as hell cured her hiccups.'

A woman comes home from the doctor.

'What did the doctor say?' her husband asks.

'He said I have the figure of an eighteen-year-old,' she replies.

'What did he say about your big fat arse,' quips the husband.

'Your name didn't come up.'

An old country doctor goes way out to the boondocks to deliver a baby. It is so far out that there is no electricity.

When the doctor arrives, no-one is home except for the labouring mother and her five-year-old child. The doctor instructs the child to hold a lantern up high so he can see while he helps the woman deliver the baby. The child does so, the mother pushes, and after a little while the doctor lifts the newborn baby by the feet and spanks him on the bottom to get him to take his first breath.

'Hit him again,' the child says. 'He shouldn't have crawled up there in the first place.'

A woman goes to her doctor for a follow-up visit after the doctor has prescribed testosterone for her. She is a little worried about some of the side effects she is experiencing.

'Doctor, the hormones you've been giving me have really helped, but I'm afraid that you're giving me too much. I've started growing hair in places that I've never grown hair before.'

The doctor reassures her. 'A little hair growth is a perfectly normal side effect of testosterone. Just where has this hair appeared?'

'On my balls.'

A man runs to the doctor and says, 'Doctor, you've got to help me. My wife thinks she's a chicken.'

The doctor says, 'How long has she had this condition?'

'Two years,' says the man.

'Then why did it take you so long to come and see me?'

The man shrugs his shoulders, 'We needed the eggs.'

An old man goes to the doctor for his yearly physical, his wife tagging along.

When the doctor enters the examination room, he tells the old man, 'I need a urine sample, a stool sample and a sperm sample.'

The old man, being hard of hearing, looks at his wife and yells, 'What? What did he say? What's he want?'

His wife yells back, 'He needs your underwear.'

A man walks into the doctor's surgery and flips his penis onto the desk and says, 'I'd like you to have a look at this Doc.'

The doctor looks and says, 'I can see nothing wrong with it.'

'I know, but it's a bloody beauty isn't it?'

Two doctors are in a hospital hallway one day complaining about Nurse Molly.

'She's incredibly mixed up,' says one doctor. 'She does everything absolutely backwards. Just last week, I told her to give a patient 2 mg of morphine every ten hours, she gave him 10 mg every two hours. He damn near died on us.'

The second doctor says, 'That's nothing. Earlier this week, I told her to give a patient an enema every twenty-four hours. She tried to give him twenty-four enemas in one hour. The guy damn near exploded.'

Suddenly they hear a bloodcurdling scream from down the hall.

'Oh my God!' says the first doctor, 'I just realised I told Nurse Molly to prick Mr Smith's boil.'

A man walks into a crowded doctor's office.

As he approaches the desk the receptionist asks, 'Yes Sir, may we help you?'

'There's something wrong with my dick,' he replies.

The receptionist is shocked and says, 'You shouldn't come into a crowded office and say things like that.'

'Why not? You asked me what was wrong and I told you,' he says.

'We do not use language like that here,' she says. 'Please go outside and come back in and say that there's something wrong with your ear or whatever.'

The man walks out, waits several minutes and re-enters. The receptionist smiles smugly and asks, 'Yes?'

'There's something wrong with my ear,' he states.

The receptionist nods approvingly.

'And what is wrong with your ear, Sir?'

'I can't bloody piss out of it,' the man replies.

An elderly married couple go to the doctor for their annual medical check-ups.

After the examination, the doctor says to the elderly man, 'You appear to be in good health. Do you have any medical concerns that you would like to discuss with me?'

'In fact, I do,' says the man. 'After I have sex with my wife for the first time, I am usually hot and sweaty. And then, after I have sex with my wife the second time, I am usually cold and chilly.'

'This is very interesting,' replies the doctor. 'Let me do some research and get back to you.'

After examining the elderly woman, the doctor says, 'Everything appears to be fine. Do you have any medical concerns that you would like to discuss with me?'

The woman replies that she has no questions or concerns. The doctor then asks, 'Your husband had an unusual concern. He claims that he is usually hot and sweaty after having sex with you the first time and then cold and chilly after the second time. Do you know why?'

'Oh that old buzzard!' she replies. 'That's because the first time is usually in summer and the second time is usually in winter.'

Queen Elizabeth II is visiting one of Australia's finest hospitals and during her tour of the wards she passes a room where one of the male patients is masturbating.

'Oh God,' says the Queen. 'That's disgraceful, what is the meaning of this?'

The doctor leading the tour explains, 'I am sorry your Royal Highness, but this man has a very serious condition where his testicles fill up rapidly with semen. If he doesn't do what he is doing at least five times per day, he could swell up and he might die.'

'Oh, I am sorry,' says the Queen. 'I was unaware that such a medical condition existed.'

On the same floor they soon pass another room where a young, blonde nurse is performing oral sex on another patient.

'Oh my God,' says the Queen. 'What's happening here?'

The doctor replies, 'Same problem, better health plan.'

A man is suffering from premature ejaculation.

'Can you do anything to help me doc?' he asks.

'No, but I can give you the address of a woman who has a short attention span.'

One day a young married couple are in their bedroom making love. All of a sudden a bumble bee enters the bedroom window. As the young woman parts her legs the bee enters her vagina.

The woman starts screaming, 'Oh my god, help me, there's a bee in my vagina.'

The husband immediately takes her to the local doctor and explains the situation.

The doctor thinks for a moment and says, 'Hmm, tricky situation. But I have a solution to the problem if young Sir will permit.'

The husband is very concerned and agrees that the doctor can use whatever method he likes to get the bee out of his wife's vagina.

The doctor says, 'OK, what I'm gonna do is rub some honey over the top of my penis and insert it into your wife's vagina. When I feel the bee getting closer to the tip of my dick I shall withdraw it and the bee should hopefully follow my penis out of your wife's vagina.'

The husband nods and gives his approval.

The young woman says, 'Yes, yes, whatever, just get on with it.'

So the doctor, after covering the tip of his penis with honey, inserts it into the young woman's vagina.

After a few gentle strokes, the doctor says, 'I don't think the bee has noticed the honey yet. Perhaps I should go a bit deeper.'

So the doctor goes deeper. After a while the doctor begins shafting the young woman very hard indeed. The young woman begins to quiver with excitement, she begins to moan and groan aloud.

'Oh doctor, doctor!' she shouts.

The doctor, concentrating very hard, looks like he is enjoying himself. He then puts his hands on the young woman's breasts and starts making loud noises.

The husband, at this point, suddenly becomes very annoyed and shouts, 'Now wait a minute, what the hell do you think you're doing?'

The doctor, still concentrating, replies, 'Change of plan, I'm gonna drown the bastard.'

Three elderly men are at the doctor's office for a memory test.

The doctor asks the first man, 'What is three times three?'

'Two hundred and seventy four,' he replies.

The doctor rolls his eyes and looks up at the ceiling, and says to the second man, 'It's your turn. What is three times three?'

'Tuesday,' replies the second man.

The doctor shakes his head sadly, then asks the third man, 'OK, your turn. What's three times three?'

'Nine,' says the third man.

'That's great!' says the doctor. 'How did you get that?'

'Simple,' he says, 'just subtract 274 from Tuesday.'

Two elderly couples are enjoying a friendly conversation when one of the men asks the other, 'Fred, how was the memory clinic you went to last month?'

'Outstanding,' Fred replies. 'They taught us all the latest psychological techniques – visualisation, association. It made a huge difference for me.'

'That's great! What was the name of the clinic?'

Fred goes blank. He thinks and thinks, but can't remember.

Then a smile breaks across his face and he asks, 'What do you call that red flower with the long stem and thorns?'

'You mean a rose?'

'Yes, that's it!' He turns to his wife. 'Rose, what was the name of that clinic?'

YOU MIGHT BE A NURSE IF...

…when using a public toilet, you wash your hands with soap for a full minute and turn off the faucets with your elbows.

…men assume you must be great in bed because of the nine billion porn movies about nurses.

…everyone, including complete strangers, tells you about each and every ache and pain they have.

…you want to put your foot through the TV screen every time you see a nurse on a soap opera doing nothing but talking on the phone and flirting with doctors.

…you can watch the goriest movie and eat anything afterwards, even spaghetti with lots of tomato sauce.

…you use a plastic 30 cc medicine cup for a shot glass.

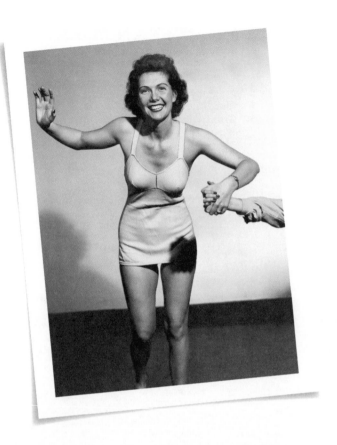

A woman has to go to the hospital unexpectedly.
She provides her husband with a list of items to bring from home. One item on her list is 'comfortable underwear'.

The husband asks, 'How will I know which ones to pick?'

'Hold them up and imagine them on me,' she answers. 'If you smile, put them back.'

A man walks into a doctor's office. He has a cucumber up his nose, a carrot in his left ear and a banana in his right ear.

'What's the matter with me?' he asks the doctor.

The doctor replies, 'You're not eating properly.'

A SHORT HISTORY OF MEDICINE

'Doctor, I have an ear ache.'

2000 B.C. : 'Here, eat this root.'

1000 B.C. : 'That root is heathen, say this prayer.'

1850 A.D. : 'That prayer is superstition, drink this potion.'

1940 A.D. : 'That potion is snake oil, swallow this pill.'

1985 A.D. : 'That pill is ineffective, take this antibiotic.'

2000 A.D. : 'That antibiotic is artificial. Here, eat this root!'

A woman, calling Mount Sinai Hospital, says, 'Hello, I want to know if a patient is getting better.'

The voice on the other end of the line says, 'What is the patient's name and room number?'

She says, 'Yes, darling! She's Sarah Finkel, in Room 302.'

The man on the phone says, 'Oh, yes. Mrs Finkel is doing very well. In fact, she's had two full meals, her blood pressure is fine, she's going to be taken off the heart monitor in a couple of hours and if she continues this improvement, Dr Cohen is going to send her home Tuesday.'

The woman says, 'Thank God! That's wonderful! Oh! That's fantastic! That's wonderful news!'

'From your enthusiasm, I take it you must be a close family member or a very close friend!'

She says, 'I'm Sarah Finkel in 302. Cohen, my doctor, doesn't tell me a word!'

An old fellow comes into the hospital, truly on death's door due to an infected gallbladder. The surgeon who removed the gallbladder is adamant that his patients be up and walking in the hall the day after surgery, to help prevent blood clots forming in the leg veins. The nurses walk the patient in the hall as ordered, and after the third day the nurse tells the

doctor how he complains bitterly each time they do.
The surgeon tells them to keep walking him.

After a week, the patient is ready to go. His children
come to pick him up and thank the surgeon profusely for
what he has done for their father. The surgeon is pleased and
appreciates the thanks, but tells them that it was really
a simple operation and he was lucky to get him in time.

'But doctor, you don't understand,' they say, 'Dad hasn't
walked in over a year!'

PATIENT: I always see spots before my eyes.
DOCTOR: Didn't the new glasses help?
PATIENT: Sure, now I see the spots much clearer.

A veterinarian is feeling ill and goes to see her doctor. The
doctor asks her all the usual questions about symptoms,
how long they have been occurring, etc.

She interrupts him, 'Hey look, I'm a vet. I don't need to ask
my patients these kinds of questions. I can tell what's wrong
just by looking. Why can't you?'

The doctor nods, looks her up and down, writes out a
prescription, and hands it to her.

'There you are. Of course, if that doesn't work, we'll have to
have you put down.'

At a medical convention, a male doctor and a female doctor
start eyeing each other. The male doctor asks the female
doctor to dinner and she accepts. As they sit down at the
restaurant, she excuses herself to go and wash her hands.

After dinner, one thing leads to another and they end up in
her hotel bedroom. Just as things get hot, the female doctor
interrupts and says she has to go and wash her hands. When
she comes back they go for it. After the sex session, she gets
up and says she is going to wash her hands.

As she comes back the male doctor says, 'I bet you are a surgeon.'
She confirms and asks how he knew.
'Easy, you're always washing your hands.'
She then says, 'I bet you're an anaesthesiologist.'
'Wow, how did you guess?' asks the male doctor.
'I didn't feel a thing.'

A girl tells her mother she played doctors with a boy in her class.
'What happened?' asks the worried mother.
'I waited 45 minutes then he billed the insurance company.'

Doctor: I've got very bad news – you've got cancer and Alzheimer's.
Patient: Well, at least I don't have cancer.

A guy has been suffering from severe headaches for years with no relief. After trying all the usual cures he's referred to a headache specialist by his family doctor. The doctor asks him what his symptoms are.

'I get these blinding headaches; kind of like a knife across my scalp and –'

He is interrupted by the doctor, 'And a heavy throbbing right behind the left ear.'

'Yes! Exactly! How did you know?'

'Well I am the world's greatest headache specialist, you know. But I myself suffered from that same type of headache for many years. It is caused by a tension in the scalp muscles. This is how I cured it: Every day I would give my wife oral sex. When she came she would squeeze her legs together with all her strength and the pressure would relieve the tension in my head. Try that every day for two weeks and come back and let me know how it goes.'

Two weeks go by and the man comes back.

'Well, how do you feel?' asks the doctor.

'Doc, I'm a new man! I feel great! I haven't had a headache since I started this treatment! I can't thank you enough. And, by the way, you have a lovely home.'

'Doc, I can't stop singing the green, green grass of home.'
'That sounds like Tom Jones syndrome.'
'Is it common?'
'It's not unusual.'

A guy walks into the psychiatrist wearing only cling-film for shorts.

The shrink says, 'Well, I can clearly see you're nuts.'

'Doc, I've got a cricket ball stuck up my backside.'
'How's that?'
'Don't you start.'

Bloke goes to the doctors with a lettuce leaf sticking out of his arse.

'Hmmmm, that's strange,' says the doctor.

Bloke replies, 'That's just the tip of the iceberg'.

Dentist: Say 'Aahh'.
Patient: Why?
Dentist: My dog's died.

A guy goes in to see a psychiatrist.

'Doc, I don't seem to be able to make any friends, so I need help from you, you fat bastard!'

A man came to hospital after a serious accident.

'Doctor, doctor, I can't feel my legs!' he shouted.

'I know you can't, I've cut your arms off.'

A man goes to the doc, with a strawberry growing out of his head.

'I'll give you some cream to put on it,' says the doctor.

Patient: Doctor, doctor, a Rottweiler bit me on the finger.
Doctor: Which one?
Patient: I don't know. All Rottweilers look the same to me.

David, a keen fisherman, had driven by a lake many times and had seen a lot of anglers pulling in plenty of fish, so he decided to give his luck a try. On his first day of fishing he had no luck at all but another fisherman near him was scooping in one fish after another. He had to know the secret.

'Excuse me sir, but would you mind telling me what sort of bait you are using?' he asked.

The other man looked around a bit embarrassed. 'Well, I am a surgeon, and quite by accident I found that human tonsils work very well.'

David thanked the surgeon and left. The next day, he returned to the lake, but still had no luck with his ordinary bait. He noticed there was another man reeling in fish after fish.

'Excuse me,' asked David, 'but could you suggest a bait that I could try?'

'Well, I can, but I am not sure it will do you any good. I'm a surgeon and I'm using a bit of human appendix.'

It seemed that the fish in this lake would require a little more effort than normal, but David was willing to give the lake one more try. On the third day, David still had no luck. There was yet another man near him bringing in fish left and right. David wanted to confirm what he already knew.

'Excuse me sir, but are you a doctor?'

'No,' replied the man. 'I'm a Rabbi.'

A man's wife has been in a coma for several days following a particularly nasty knock on the head. As usual, one of the nurses in the hospital is giving her a wash in bed. As she washes down the woman's body, she sponges her pubic hair. Out of the corner of her eye the nurse thinks she has seen the woman's eyebrows shudder. Not quite sure, she tries again. This time, she actually does see some movement.

'Doctor, Doctor,' she calls, 'I saw some movement!'

The Doctor comes into the room and tries as well. Once more, they both see movement around the woman's eyes.

'Well this is good news,' says the doctor. 'I think we should call her husband and let him know.'

They call her husband and tell him that they have seen some movement. When he arrives, they explain that by touching the woman's pubic hair, they were seeing some sort of reaction in her facial muscles. The doctor suggests that the husband might like to try something a little more adventurous in order to provoke a stronger reaction.

'I suggest that we leave the room and that you try a little oral sex,' he says.

The husband agrees and is left alone in the room. Several moments later, all the emergency alarms and buzzers are activated. The doctor and a host of nurses run into the wife's room where they see the husband zipping up his jeans.

'Oops,' he says, 'I think I choked her.'

How many triage nurses does it take to change a light bulb?

One, but the bulb will have to spend four hours in the waiting room.

'Doctor, doctor, my hands are killing me.'
'Take them off your throat.'

'Doctor, doctor, how long have I got?'
'Ten.'
'Ten what? Ten months? Ten weeks?'
'Ten, nine, eight, seven...'

'Doctor, doctor, have you got something for a migraine?'
'Take this hammer and hit yourself on the head.'

A man takes his Rottweiler to the vet and says to him, 'My dog's cross-eyed. Is there anything you can do for it?'

'Well,' says the vet, 'let's have a look at him.'

So he picks the dog up by the ears and has a good look at its eyes.

'I'm going to have to put him down,' says the vet.

'Just because he's cross-eyed?' says the man.

'No, because he's heavy,' says the vet.

A certain zoo has acquired a female of a very rare species of gorilla. Within a few weeks, the gorilla becomes very difficult to handle. Upon examination, the zoo veterinarian determines the problem. The gorilla is on heat. To make matters worse, there are no male gorillas available. While reflecting on their problem, the zoo administrators notice Paul, an employee responsible for cleaning the animals' cages. Paul, it is rumoured, possesses ample ability to satisfy any female, but he isn't very bright. So, the zoo administrators think they might have a solution. Paul is approached with a proposition. Would he be willing to screw the gorilla for $500? Paul shows some interest, but says he will have to think the matter over carefully. The following day, Paul announces that he will accept their offer, but only on three conditions.

'First,' he says, 'I don't want to kiss her. Secondly, I want nothing to do with any offspring that may result from this union.'

The zoo administration quickly agrees to these conditions, so they ask for his third condition.

'Well,' says Paul, 'you've gotta give me another week to come up with the $500.'

DOCTOR: Ma'am, are you sexually active?
WOMAN: Well, sometimes…and sometimes I just lie there.

Hello, and welcome to the mental health hotline.

If you are obsessive-compulsive, press one repeatedly.

If you are co-dependent, please ask someone to press two for you.

If you have multiple personalities, press three, four, five and six.

If you are paranoid, we know who you are and what you want. Stay on the line so we can trace your call.

If you are delusional, press seven and your call will be transferred to the mother ship.

If you are schizophrenic, listen carefully and a small voice will tell you which number to press.

If you are manic depressive, it doesn't matter which number you press, no one will answer.

If you have a nervous disorder, please fidget with the hash key until someone comes on the line.

If you are dyslexic, press 6969696969.

If you have amnesia, press eight and state your name, address, phone number, date of birth, social security number, and your mother's maiden name.

If you have post-traumatic-stress disorder, slowly and carefully press 000.

If you have bipolar disorder, please leave a message after the beep, or before the beep, or after the beep. Please wait for the beep.

If you have short-term memory loss, press nine. If you have short-term memory loss, press nine. If you have short-term memory loss, press nine. If you have short-term memory loss, press nine.

If you have low self-esteem, please hang up. All our operators are too busy to talk to you.

A psychiatrist is conducting a group therapy session with three young mothers and their small children.

'You all have obsessions,' he observes.

To the first mother he says, 'You are obsessed with eating. You've even named your daughter Candy.'

He turns to the second mum. 'Your obsession is money. Again, it manifests itself in your child's name, Penny.'

At this point, the third mother gets up, takes her little boy by the hand and whispers, 'Come on, Dick, let's go.'

A man goes to a psychologist and says, 'I got a real problem, I can't stop thinking about sex.'

The psychologist says, 'Well let's see what we can find out.'

He pulls out his ink blots. 'What is this a picture of?' he asks.

The man turns the picture upside down then turns it around and states, 'That's a man and a woman on a bed making love.'

The psychologist says, 'Very interesting,' and shows him the next picture. 'And what is this a picture of?'

The man looks and turns it in different directions and says, 'That's a man and a woman on a bed making love.'

The psychologist tries again with a third ink blot, and asks the same question, 'What is this a picture of?'

The patient again turns it in all directions and replies, 'That's a man and a woman on a bed making love.'

The psychologist states, 'Well, yes, you do seem to be obsessed with sex.'

'Me?' demands the patient. 'You're the one who keeps showing me the dirty pictures.'

A distraught man goes to see a psychologist.

'How may I help you?' the therapist asks.

'Every night I have the same dream. I'm lying in bed and a dozen women walk in and try to rip my clothes off and have wild sex with me.'

'And then what do you do?' the psychologist asks.

'I push them away,' the man says.

'Then what do you want me to do?' the psychologist asks.

'Break my arms!'

A wife goes to see a therapist and says, 'I've got a big problem, doctor. Every time we're in bed and my husband climaxes, he lets out an ear-splitting yell.'

'My dear,' the doctor says, 'that's completely natural. I don't see what the problem is.'

'The problem is,' she complains, 'it wakes me up!'

A young woman goes to her doctor complaining of pain.

'Where are you hurting?' asks the doctor.

'I hurt all over,' says the woman.

'What do you mean, all over?' asks the doctor. 'Be a little more specific.'

The woman touches her right knee with her index finger and yells, 'Ow, that hurts.'

Then she touches her left cheek and again yells, 'Ouch! That hurts, too.'

Then she touches her right earlobe.

'Ow, even that hurts,' she cries.

The doctor checks her thoughtfully for a moment and tells her his diagnosis, 'You have a broken finger.'

HISTORY NEVER REPEATS...

This is a compilation of answers by American history students.

1 Ancient Egypt was inhabited by mummies and they all wrote in hydraulics. They lived in the Sarah Dessert and travelled by Camelot. The climate of the Sarah is such that the inhabitants have to live elsewhere.

2 Moses led the Hebrew slaves to the Red Sea, where they made unleavened bread which is bread made without any ingredients. Moses went up on Mount Cyanide to get the Ten Commandments. He died before he ever reached Canada.

3 Actually, Homer was not written by Homer but by another man of that name.

4 Socrates was a famous Greek teacher who went around giving people advice. They killed him. Socrates died from an overdose of wedlock. After his death, his career suffered a dramatic decline.

5 Joan of Arc was burnt to a steak and was canonised by Bernard Shaw. Finally Magna Carta provided that no man should be hanged twice for the same offence.

6 In midevil times most people were alliterate. The greatest writer of the futile ages was Chaucer, who wrote many poems and verses and also wrote literature.

7 Another story was William Tell, who shot an arrow through an apple while standing on his son's head.

8 It was an age of great inventions and discoveries. Gutenberg invented removable type and the bible. Another important invention was the circulation of blood. Sir Walter Raleigh is a historical figure because he invented cigarettes and started smoking. And Sir Francis Drake circumcised the world with a 100-foot clipper.

9 The greatest writer of the Renaissance was William Shakespeare. He was born in the year 1564, supposedly on his birthday. He never made much money and is famous only because of his plays. He wrote tragedies, comedies and hysterectomies, all in Islamic pentameter. Romeo and Juliet are an example of a heroic couplet.

10 Writing at the same time as Shakespeare was Miguel Cervantes. He wrote Donkey Hote. The next great author was John Milton. Milton wrote Paradise Lost. Then his wife died and he wrote Paradise Regained.

11 During the Renaissance America began. Christopher Columbus was a great navigator who discovered America while cursing about the Atlantic. His ships were called the Nina, the Pinta and the Santa Fe.

12 Abraham Lincoln became America's greatest Precedent. Lincoln's mother died in infancy, and he was born in a log cabin which he built with his own hands. Abraham Lincoln freed the slaves by signing the Emasculation Proclamation. On the night of 14 April 1865, Lincoln went to the theatre and got shot in his seat by one of the actors in a moving picture show. The believed assassinator was John Wilkes Booth, a supposedly insane actor. This ruined Booth's career.

13 Gravity was invented by Issac Walton. It is chiefly noticeable in the autumn when the apples are falling off the trees.

14 Johann Bach wrote a great many musical compositions and had a large number of children. In between he practised on an old spinster which he kept up in his attic. Bach died from 1750 to the present. Bach was the most famous composer in the world and so was Handel. Handel was half German half Italian and half English. He was very large.

15 Beethoven wrote music even though he was deaf. He was so deaf he wrote loud music. He took long walks in the forest even when everyone was calling for him. Beethoven expired in 1827 and later died for this.

16 The sun never set on the British Empire because the British Empire's in the East and the sun sets in the West.

17 Queen Victoria was the longest queen. She sat on a thorn for sixty-three years. She was a moral woman who practised virtue. Her death was the final event which ended her reign.

18 Louis Pasteur discovered a cure for rabbis. Charles Darwin was a naturalist who wrote the Organ of the Species. Madman Curie discovered radio. And Karl Marx became one of the Marx brothers.

19 The First World War, caused by the assignation of the Arch-Duck by an anarchist, ushered in a new error in the anals of human history.

JAIL JOKES

A wife wakes in the middle of the night to find her husband missing from bed. She gets out of bed and checks around the house. She hears sobbing from the cellar. After turning on the light and descending the stairs, she finds her husband curled up in a little ball, sobbing.

'Honey, what's wrong?' she asks, worried about what could have hurt him so much.

'Remember, twenty years ago, I got you pregnant? And your father said I had to marry you or go to jail?'

'Yes, of course,' she replies.

'Well, today I would have been a free man.'

Two young guys are picked up by the cops for smoking dope and appear in court before the judge.

The judge says, 'You seem like nice young men, and I'd like to give you a second chance rather than jail time. I want you to go out this weekend and try to show others the evils of drug use and get them to give up drugs forever. I'll see you back in court Monday.'

On Monday, the two guys are back in court, and the judge says to the first one, 'How did you do over the weekend?'

'Well, Your Honour, I persuaded seventeen people to give up drugs forever.'

'Seventeen people? That's wonderful. What did you tell them?'

'I used a diagram, Your Honour. I drew two circles like this and told them this big circle is your brain before drugs and this small circle is your brain after drugs.'

'That's admirable. And you, how did you do?' the judge asks the second boy.

'Well, Your Honour, I persuaded 150 people to give up drugs forever.'

'One hundred and fifty people! That's amazing! How did you manage to do that?'

'Well, I used a similar approach. I said, This small circle is your arsehole before prison…'

Three frogs are arrested and brought into the courtroom for sentencing. The judge asks the first frog, 'What's your name?'

'Frog.'

'What were you arrested for?'

'Blowing bubbles in the water.'

Then he asks the second frog, 'What's your name?'

'Frog.'

'What were you arrested for?'

'Blowing bubbles in the water.'

Then he asks the third frog, 'What's your name?'

'Bubbles.'

JAIL VS WORK

IN PRISON...you spend the majority of your time in a 3 m × 3 m cell.

AT WORK...you spend the majority of your time in a 2 m × 2 m cubicle.

IN PRISON...you get three meals a day.

AT WORK...you only get a break for one meal and you pay for it.

IN PRISON...you get time off for good behaviour

AT WORK...you get more work for good behaviour

IN PRISON...the guard locks and unlocks all the doors for you.

AT WORK...you must carry around a security card and open all the doors for yourself.

IN PRISON...you can watch TV and play games.

AT WORK...you get fired for watching TV and playing games.

IN PRISON…you get your own toilet.
AT WORK…you have to share with some idiot who pees on the seat.

IN PRISON…they allow your family and friends to visit.
AT WORK…you can't even speak to your family.

IN PRISON…the taxpayers pay all expenses with no work required.
AT WORK…you get to pay all the expenses to go to work and then they deduct taxes from your salary to pay for prisoners.

IN PRISON…you spend most of your life inside bars wanting to get out.
AT WORK…you spend most of your time wanting to get out and go inside bars.

IN PRISON…you must deal with sadistic wardens.
AT WORK…they are called managers.

CULTURAL DIVERSITY

Norman marries an upper class English girl. On their wedding night, he can't wait to get it on. He takes his clothes off, jumps into bed, and starts groping his new bride. She is both shocked and unimpressed.

'Norman, I expect you to be as polite in bed as you are at the dinner table,' she says.

Norman folds his hands on his lap, 'Is this better?'

'Much better!' she replies smiling.

'OK, then,' he says, 'now, will you please pass the pussy?'

Three guys are on a trip to Saudi Arabia. One day, they stumble into a harem tent filled with over 100 beautiful women. They start getting friendly with all the women, when suddenly the sheik comes in.

'I am the master of all these women. No-one else can touch them except me. You three men must pay for what you have done today. You will be punished in a way corresponding to your profession.'

The sheik turns to the first man and asks him what he does for a living.

'I'm a cop,' says the first man.

'Then we will shoot your penis off,' says the sheik. He then turns to the second man and asks him what he does for a living.

'I'm a fireman,' says the second man.

'Then we will burn your penis off,' says the sheik.

Finally, he asks the last man, 'And you, what do you do for a living?'

The third man answers, with a massive grin, 'I'm a lollipop salesman!'

An Englishman, an Irishman and a Scotsman have been working as jackaroos out west for many months, and are feeling the need of a woman. They therefore get together and acquire, by mail order from Canberra, an inflatable sex doll. They draw lots, and the Englishman gets the first shot.

Half an hour or so later, he comes out of the spare room with a smile on his face.

'Bloody great is that! Better than the wife any day!'

Encouraged, the Scotsman goes in, and emerges after a few minutes with a grin. 'Yer nae bloody wrong, Jimmy. It was worth the cost o' a pint.'

The Irishman takes his turn, and emerges after only a short while with a puzzled and frustrated frown. 'Oi don't know what youse was raving on about. It's bloody useless! All Oi did was give her a little love bite, and she lets out a bloody great fart and flies out the window.'

A Texan lands in Sydney, and is picked up by a taxi. After requesting a tour of the city, he starts into a tirade about the small-town airport and how in Texas they have larger runways on their ranches.

They are soon crossing the Sydney Harbour Bridge, and the Texan is further unimpressed, 'I have a duck pond bigger than that harbour, and an ornamental bridge to span it that makes this look like a toy.'

The Sydney-Newcastle Expressway also gets his scorn. 'Is this a road, or a track?' he shouts with contempt.

So when a kangaroo jumps out in front of the cab, causing the sudden and severe application of the brakes, the driver can't help himself.

'Bloody grasshoppers!' he says.

A twelve-year-old boy goes up to his Irish neighbour and says, 'I was looking in your bedroom window last night and I saw your wife giving you a blow job. Nyah, nyah, nyah.'

The Irish guy laughs and answers, 'The joke's on you, Johnny. Nyah, nyah, nyah – I wasn't even home last night.'

The National Transportation Safety Board recently divulged that they had funded a project with American car-makers over the past five years. In the covert project, car-makers installed black boxes in 4WD pick-up trucks in an effort to determine, in fatal accidents, the circumstances in the last fifteen seconds before the crash.

They were surprised to find in forty-nine of the fifty states the last words of drivers in 61.2% of fatal crashes were, 'Oh, shit!'

Only the state of Texas was different. There, 89.3% of the final words were, 'Hey y'all, hold my beer and watch this!'

IN THE AIR

A military cargo plane, flying over a populated area, suddenly loses power and starts to nose dive. The pilot tries to pull up, but with all their cargo, the plane is too heavy. He yells to the soldiers in the back to throw things out to make the plane lighter. They throw out a pistol.

'Throw out more!' shouts the pilot. So they throw out a rifle.

'More!' he cries again. They heave out a missile. The plane stabilises and the pilot regains control. With a sigh of relief they land safely at the airport.

They unload the plane and head off home. Pretty soon they meet a boy on the side of the road who's crying. They stop and ask why he is crying.

'I was riding my bike and out of the sky a pistol hit me on the head!'

They drive a little further, and meet a boy who's crying even harder. Again they stop and ask why the boy crying.

He says, 'I was walking to the shops when from nowhere a rifle hit me on the head!'

They keep driving until they come across a boy who is crying hysterically. They stop and ask him what the matter is.

'Nothing,' the boy replies, 'I'm crying from laughter. I just farted and a house blew up!'

NASA planned a mission that involved keeping three astronauts in space for two years. Because of the extended duration of the trip, each was allowed to take 100 kg of baggage.

The first astronaut decided to take along his wife. The second decided to take along tapes so he could learn how to speak Arabic. The third astronaut decided to take along 800 packets of cigarettes.

Two years later, when the space shuttle landed, there was a big crowd waiting to welcome them home. Out came the first astronaut and his wife, each with a baby in their arms. Next, came the second astronaut speaking fluent Arabic. They both gave their speeches and got a rousing applause.

Suddenly out came the third astronaut with a cigarette in his mouth. He walked up to the podium and snarled at the crowd, 'Has anyone got a match?'

An elderly doctor and a Baptist minister are seated next to each other on a plane. The plane is delayed on the ground due to some technical problems. Just after taking off, the pilot offers his apologies to the passengers and announces that a round of free drinks will be served.

When the charming flight attendant comes round with her trolley, the doctor orders a gin and tonic for himself. The flight attendant then asks the minister whether he wants anything.

He replies, 'Oh no! Thank you. I would rather commit adultery than drink alcohol.'

The elderly doctor promptly hands his gin and tonic back to the flight attendant and says, 'Madam, I did not know there was a choice.'

A student was heading home for the holidays. When she got to the airline counter, she presented her ticket to Houston. 'I'd like you to send my green suitcase to Hawaii, and my red suitcase to London,' she told the agent.

The confused agent said, 'I'm sorry, we can't to that.'

'Really? I am so relieved to hear you say that because that's exactly what you did with my luggage last year!'

What's the difference between a skydiver and a golfer? A golfer goes 'WHACK! … Oh shit!' A skydiver goes 'Oh shit!…WHACK!'

SOME QUICKIES

What do you get when you cross LSD with birth control?
A trip without the kids.

What do you call a beautiful, sunny day that comes after
two cloudy, rainy ones?
Monday.

Why did the chicken lawyer cross the road?
To get to the car accident on the other side.

Why do birds fly south?
Because it's too far to walk.

What is the difference between a cat and a comma?
One has the paws before the claws and the other has the clause before the pause.

What has four legs and an arm?
A happy pit bull.

What colour is a hiccup?
Burple.

Why did the cannibal live on his own?
He'd had his fill of other people.

Why do women have breasts?
So men will talk to them!

Did you hear about the idiot who walked around the world?
He drowned.

What's the difference between Monica Lewinsky and the rest of us?
When we want some dick in the white house, we just vote.

What is the difference between a statistician and an accountant?
A statistician is someone who is good with numbers but lacks the personality to be an accountant.

MISCELLANEOUS

One day an out-of-work mime visits the zoo and attempts to earn some money as a street performer. Unfortunately, as soon as he starts to draw a crowd, a zookeeper grabs him and drags him into his office.

He thinks he is in trouble, but in fact, the zookeeper explains to the mime that the zoo's most popular attraction, a gorilla, has died suddenly and the keeper fears that attendance at the zoo will fall off. He offers the mime a job to dress up as the gorilla and play the role until they can get another one.

The mime accepts and the next morning he puts on a gorilla suit and enters the cage before the crowd arrives.

He discovers that it's a great job. He can sleep all he wants, play and make fun of people, and he draws bigger crowds than he ever did as a mime.

However, eventually the crowds get bored with him and he tires of just swinging around on tyres. He begins to notice that the people are paying more attention to the lion in the cage next to his. Not wanting to lose the attention of his audience, he climbs to the top of his cage, crawls across a partition, and dangles from the top to the lion's cage. Of course, this makes the lion furious, but the crowd loves it.

At the end of the day the zookeeper comes and gives the mime a raise for being such a good attraction. This goes on for some time. The mime keeps taunting the lion, the crowds grow larger, and his salary keeps going up.

Then one terrible day when he is dangling over the furious lion he slips and falls. The mime is terrified. The lion gathers itself and prepares to pounce. The mime is so scared that he begins to run round and round the cage with the lion close behind.

Finally, the mime starts screaming and yelling, 'Help, Help me!', but the lion is quick and pounces. The mime soon finds himself flat on his back looking up at the angry lion and the lion says, 'Shut up you idiot! Do you want to get us both fired?'

SIGNS YOU HAVE HAD
TOO MUCH OF MODERN LIFE

- You buy a computer and a week later it is out of date…and now sells for half the price you paid.
- You exchange emails several times a day with a stranger from South Africa, but you haven't spoken to your next door neighbour this year.
- You consider second-day air delivery painfully slow.
- You have a list of fifteen phone numbers to reach your family of three.
- You haven't played solitaire with a real deck of cards in years.
- Your reason for not staying in touch with family is that they do not have email addresses.

Five quotes for married men:

1 I married Miss Right. I just didn't know her first name was Always.

2 It isn't true that married men live longer than single men. It only seems longer.

3 Losing a wife can be hard. In my case, it was almost impossible.

4 A man is incomplete until he is married. After that, he is finished.

5 I haven't spoken to my wife for 18 months. I don't like to interrupt her.

TELEMARKETER TORTURE

What to do when your dinner is interrupted by a keen telemarketer on the phone:

Go absolutely silent.

Breathe slowly and heavily into the phone.

Mumble: 'I like to watch.'

Pretend that this is a call that you are expecting from the child psychologist in relation to your troubled and disruptive teenage son.

Ask them if they are selling beer.

Start speaking in another language.

Tell them the person they want doesn't live here anymore.

Give them the number of a phone sex line and tell them that it is the new number.

Tell them that you're not here right now.

Start selling them something else.

Tell them you're poor and ask for money.

Start preaching your religion to them.

Try to hypnotise them.

Put on some really annoying music and put the phone up to the stereo.

Ask the telemarketer if s/he is single. Then try hitting on him/her. Be sure to mention your various medical problems and your fascination with odd smells.

Use a voice changer to disguise your voice.

Rap all your replies to the telemarketer's questions.

Ask the telemarketer if s/he minds if you talk to him/her on the toilet. Then take a plastic sauce bottle and squeeze out sauce repeatedly.

Try to rhyme with everything the telemarketer says.

Sell them on the 'value of high colonics'. Explain your 'dedication to good health' in your most convincing, passionate voice.

Start talking about your many medical ailments and don't allow the telemarketer to get a word in.

DOMESTIC TIPS

Smell gas? Locate the suspected leak by striking an ordinary match in every room in the house until a loud explosion reveals the source of the escaping gas.

To stop nose bleeds, simply place your head between your knees until your heart stops.

When you leave the house simply plug the phone into your video recorder. Not only will it record the caller's voice, but you will also get a picture of them speaking, probably.

Transform your garage into a drive-through restaurant by sitting in your car, lowering your window and demanding that your wife brings you a cup of tea, on roller skates.

Pretend to be Welsh by putting coal dust behind your ears, talking gibberish and singing all the time.

If a small child is choking on an ice cube, don't panic. Simply pour a jug of boiling water down its throat and hey presto! The blockage is almost instantly removed.

Save electricity on freezing winter nights by simply unplugging your fridge and placing the contents of it on your doorstep.

Help the local police by popping into the mortuary every day to see if you can identify any of the bodies.

Avoid the morning-after hangover – simply stay drunk past noon.

Brighten up dull Monday mornings at work by concealing a bottle of vodka in your jacket pocket and taking swigs from it at regular intervals throughout the day.

Are you sick and tired of using the same jokes over and over? Why not send them in to be recycled? You'll be saving lots of hot air that would have otherwise effected global warming.

Housewives: When nipping out to the shops, remember to carry a stiff broom in the boot of your car. Use it to sweep the broken glass to the side of the road every time you have a minor accident.

Bomb disposal experts' wives: Keep hubby on his toes by packing his lunchbox with plasticine and an old alarm clock.

Bus drivers: Pretend you are an airline pilot by wedging your accelerator pedal down with a heavy book, securing the steering wheel with some old rope, and then strolling back along the bus chatting casually to the passengers.

X-Files fans: Create the effect of being abducted by aliens by drinking two bottles of vodka. You'll invariably wake up in a strange place the following morning, having had your memory mysteriously 'erased'.

Increase blind people's electricity bills by switching all their lights on when their guide dog isn't looking.

A woman walks into a supermarket and loads up her trolley with the following items:

1 bar of soap
1 toothbrush
1 tube of toothpaste
1 loaf of bread
1 pint of milk
1 single serving of cereal
1 single-serve frozen dinner
1 can of Soup For One
1 can of light beer

The guy at the check-out looks at her and says, 'Single, are you?'

The woman smiles sweetly and replies, 'How did you guess?'

'Because you're ugly.'

SIGNS COLLECTED BY A FLIGHT ATTENDANT ALONG HER TRAVELS

The sign in a Norwegian lounge reads: LADIES ARE REQUESTED NOT TO HAVE CHILDREN IN THE BAR

A hotel notice in Madrid informs: IF YOU WISH DISINFECTION ENACTED IN YOUR PRESENCE, PLEASE CRY OUT FOR THE CHAMBERMAID

In the window of a Swedish furrier the message reads: FUR COATS MADE FOR LADIES FROM THEIR OWN SKIN

The room service in a Lisbon hotel tells you: IF YOU WISH FOR BREAKFAST, LIFT THE TELEPHONE AND ASK FOR ROOM SERVICE. THIS WILL BE ENOUGH FOR YOU TO BRING YOUR FOOD UP

A Polish hotel informs prospective visitors in a flyer: AS FOR THE TROUT SERVED YOU AT THE HOTEL MONOPOL, YOU WILL BE SINGING ITS PRAISE TO YOUR GRANDCHILDREN AS YOU LIE ON YOUR DEATHBED

A Seville tailor makes clear how he will handle commissions: ORDER NOW YOUR SUMMER SUIT, BECAUSE IS BIG RUSH WE WILL EXECUTE CUSTOMERS IN STRICT ROTATION

A dentist's doorway in Istanbul proclaims: AMERICAN DENTIST, 2TH FLOOR. TEETH EXTRACTED BY LATEST METHODISTS.

Some German hospitals now display the sign: NO CHILDREN ALLOWED IN THE MATERNITY WARDS

A Roman doctor proclaims himself a: SPECIALIST IN WOMEN AND OTHER DISEASES

A sign in a Kowloon hotel warns: IS FORBIDDEN TO STEAL HOTEL TOWELS. PLEASE IF YOU ARE NOT PERSON TO DO SUCH IS PLEASE NOT TO READ NOTICE.

Visitors in a Czechoslovakian tourist agency are invited to: TAKE ONE OF OUR HORSE-DRIVEN CITY TOURS – WE GUARANTEE NO MISCARRIAGES

A sign posted in Germany's Black Forest reads: IT IS STRICTLY FORBIDDEN ON OUR BLACK FOREST CAMPING SITE THAT PEOPLE OF DIFFERENT SEX, FOR INSTANCE, MEN AND WOMEN, LIVE TOGETHER IN ONE TENT UNLESS THEY ARE MARRIED WITH EACH OTHER FOR THAT PURPOSE

A notice in a Vienna hotel urges: IN CASE OF FIRE DO YOUR UTMOST TO ALARM THE HALL PORTER

On a Paris hotel elevator: PLEASE LEAVE YOUR VALUES AT THE FRONT DESK

In an Athens hotel: VISITORS ARE EXPECTED TO COMPLAIN AT THE OFFICE BETWEEN 9 A.M. AND 11 A.M. DAILY

On a Belgrade elevator: TO MOVE THE CABIN, PUSH BUTTON FOR WISHING FLOOR. IF THE CABIN SHOULD ENTER MORE PERSONS, EACH ONE SHOULD PRESS A NUMBER OF WISHING FLOOR. DRIVING IS THEN GOING ALPHABETICALLY BY NATIONAL ORDER.

In a Japanese hotel: YOU ARE INVITED TO TAKE ADVANTAGE OF THE CHAMBERMAID

In a Moscow hotel: YOU ARE WELCOME TO VISIT THE CEMETERY WHERE FAMOUS RUSSIAN AND SOVIET COMPOSERS, ARTISTS AND WRITERS ARE BURIED DAILY EXCEPT THURSDAY

On a Swiss menu: OUR WINES LEAVE YOU NOTHING TO HOPE FOR

On a Polish menu: SALAD A FIRM'S OWN MAKE; LIMPID RED BEET SOUP WITH CHEESY DUMPLINGS IN THE FORM OF A FINGER ROASTED DUCK LET LOOSE; BEEF RASHERS BEATEN UP IN THE COUNTRY PEOPLE'S FASHION.

In a Bangkok dry-cleaners: DROP YOUR TROUSERS HERE FOR BEST RESULTS

In a Paris dress shop: DRESSES FOR STREET WALKING

In a Soviet newspaper: THERE WILL BE A MOSCOW EXHIBITION OF ART BY 16 000 SOVIET REPUBLIC PAINTERS AND SCULPTORS. THESE WERE EXECUTED OVER THE PAST TWO YEARS.

At a Swiss mountain inn: SPECIAL TODAY – NO ICE CREAM

At a Tokyo car rental firm: WHEN PASSENGER OF FOOT HAVE IN SIGHT, TOOTLE THE HORN. TRUMPET HIM MELODIOUSLY AT FIRST, BUT IF HE STILL OBSTACLES YOUR PASSAGE THEN TOOTLE HIM WITH VIGOUR.

In a Majorcan shop: ENGLISH WELL TALKING. HERE SPEECHING AMERICAN.

DOGS VS CATS

What is a dog?

1 Dogs lie around all day, sprawled on the most comfortable piece of furniture.
2 They can hear a package of food opening half a block away, but don't hear you when you're in the same room.
3 They can look dumb and lovable all at the same time.
4 When you want to play, they want to play.
5 When you want to be alone, they want to play.
6 They are great at begging.
7 They do disgusting things with their mouths and then try to give you a kiss.

Conclusion: Dogs are tiny men in little fur coats.

What is a cat?

1 Cats do what they want, and they rarely listen to you.
2 They're totally unpredictable and moody.
3 They whine when they are not happy.
4 When you want to play, they want to be alone.
5 When you want to be alone, they want to play.
6 They expect you to cater to their every whim.
7 They drive you nuts and cost an arm and a leg.

Conclusion: Cats are tiny women in little fur coats.

LAST LAUGHS...

Dear Linda,
I have no doubt you understand that I have certain needs that you, being 57 years old, cannot satisfy. I am happy with you and I value you as a good wife and I hope you will not wrongly interpret the fact that I will be spending the evening with my 19-year-old personal assistant at a hotel. Please don't be upset, I will be home before midnight.

When the man came home late that night he found a reply on the dining room table:

Dear Jeff,

I received your letter and I wish to thank you for your honesty. I would like to remind you that you are also 57 years old. As you know, I am a university lecturer. I would like to inform you that while you read this, I will be at a hotel with Andre, one of my students. He is young, virile and like your personal assistant, he is 19 years old. You, being a successful businessman who is good with numbers, will surely understand that we are in the same situation, although with one small difference: 19 goes into 57 a lot more times than 57 goes into 19. Therefore, I will not be home until sometime tomorrow.

An Irishman walks into a pub and asks for three pints of Guinness. The bartender brings him three pints. The man takes alternate sips of each one until they're gone. He then orders three more.

'Sir, you don't have to order three at a time. I can keep an eye on it and when you get low I'll bring you a fresh cold one,' says the bartender.

'You don't understand,' says the Irishman. 'I have two brothers, one in Australia and one in the States. We made a vow to each other that every Saturday night we'd still drink together. So right now, my brothers have three Guinness stouts too, and we're drinking together.'

The bartender thought that was a wonderful tradition. And so every week the man came in and ordered three beers. Then one week he came in and ordered only two. He drank them and then ordered two more.

'I know your tradition and I'd just like to say that I'm sorry that one of your brothers died,' said the bartender.

'Oh, me brothers are fine. I just quit drinking.'

A squad car driver was covering a quiet beat out in the sticks, when he was amazed to find a former police lieutenant covering the same beat.

He stopped the car and asked, 'Why, Smithson, this wouldn't be your new beat way out here in the sticks, would it?'

'That it is,' Smithson replied grimly, 'ever since I arrested Judge O'Shea on his way to the masquerade ball.'

'You mean you pinched his honour?'

'How was I to know that his convict suit was only a costume?'

'Well, that's life. There's a lesson in here somewhere. '

'That there is,' replied Smithson. 'Never book a judge by his cover.'

Sherlock Holmes and Dr Watson go camping, and pitch their tent under the stars.

During the night, Holmes wakes his companion and says, 'Watson, look up at the stars, and tell me what you deduce.'

Watson says, 'I see millions of stars, and even if a few of those have planets, it's quite likely there are some planets like earth, and if there are a few planets like earth out there, there might also be life.'

Holmes replies, 'Watson, you idiot. Somebody stole our tent.'

Three dead bodies turn up at the mortuary, all with very big smiles on their faces. The coroner calls the police to tell them the causes of death.

'First body: Frenchman, 60, died of heart failure while making love to his mistress. Hence the enormous smile,' says the coroner.

'Second body: Scotsman, 25, won a thousand dollars on the lottery, spent it all on whisky. Died of alcohol poisoning, hence the smile.'

'What of the third body?' asks the inspector.

'Ah, this is the most unusual one: Billy-Bob, the country lad from Oklahoma, 30, struck by lightning.'

'Why is he smiling then?'

'Thought he was having his picture taken.'

Deep within a forest a little turtle begins to climb a tree. After hours of effort he reaches the top, jumps into the air waving his front legs and crashes to the ground. After recovering, he slowly climbs the tree again, jumps, and falls to the ground.

The turtle tries again and again while a couple of birds sitting on a branch watch his sad efforts. Finally, the female bird turns to her mate.

'Dear,' she chirps, 'I think it's time to tell him he's adopted.'

Two little boys are watching TV with their parents. The mother looks over at the father with a wink and a nod towards the upstairs bedroom. The father nods.

The mother turns to the sons and says, 'We're going upstairs for a while. You two stay here and watch TV, we'll be right back, all right?'

The two boys nod and the parents run upstairs.

The older boy is suspicious and tiptoes up the stairs.

He goes back down, shaking his head with disapproval.

'Come with me', he says to his little brother.

As the two boys tiptoe up the stairs, the older brother says, 'Now I want you to keep in mind that this is the same woman who used to kick our arses for sucking our thumbs.'

An English anthropologist is doing research in an isolated African village, and the tribal chief asks if he would like to attend a trial his people are conducting that afternoon.

'You'll be surprised,' says the chief, 'at how well we've copied your country's legal procedures. You see, we have read accounts of many English trials in your newspapers, and incorporated them into our judicial system.'

When the Englishman arrives at the wooden courthouse, he is truly amazed to see how closely the African court officials resemble those in England. The counsels are suitably attired in long black robes and the traditional white powdered wigs. Each argues his case with eloquence and in proper judicial language.

But he can't help being puzzled by the occasional appearance of a bare-breasted native woman running through the crowd waving her arms frantically.

After the trial, the anthropologist congratulates his host on what he has seen and then asks, 'What was the purpose of having a semi-nude woman run through the courtroom during the trial?'

'I really don't know,' confesses the chief, 'but in all the accounts we read in your papers about British trials, there was invariably something about "an excited titter running through the gallery" so we did our best.'

Barty was trapped in a bog and seemed a goner when Big Mick O'Reilly wandered by.

'Help!' Barty shouted, 'Oi'm sinkin'!'

'Don't worry,' reassured Mick. 'Next to the Strong Muldoon, Oi'm the strongest man in Erin, and Oi'll pull ye right out o' there.'

Mick leaned out and grabbed Barty's hand and pulled and pulled to no avail.

After two more unsuccessful attempts, Mick said to Barty, 'Shure, an' Oi can't do it. The Strong Muldoon could do it alone, mebbe, but Oi'll have to get some help.'

'Mick! Mick! D'ye think it will help if Oi pull me feet out of the stirrups?'

One night a man breaks into a house and is in the middle of stealing the home entertainment centre, when out of nowhere he hears, 'Jesus is watching.'

This totally spooks him so he searches around with his torch. Up in the corner he finds a birdcage with a parrot inside.

Relieved, he says, 'Pretty Polly,' to which the parrot replies, 'Jesus is watching.'

The thief asks the bird what his name is and the bird says 'Moses.'

The thief says, 'What a silly name for a bird.'

The bird replies, 'You think that's funny, the Rottweiler's name is Jesus.'

NEIGHBOUR: What are you up to there, Tommy?
TOMMY: My goldfish died and I've just buried him.
NEIGHBOUR: That's an awfully big hole for a goldfish, isn't it?
TOMMY: That's because he's inside your stupid cat.

A nationwide search is held for the country's best poet.
There is pretty stiff competition but eventually it comes down to two finalists – one a Yale graduate, the other a country lad.

The final contest is for them to write a poem in two minutes containing the word Timbuktu.

The Yale graduate recites his poem first.

Slowly across the desert sand
Trekked a lonely caravan.
Men on camels two by two
Destination Timbuktu.

The audience goes wild. They think the country lad doesn't stand a chance. Nevertheless, he stands up and recites his poem.

Me and Tim a-hunting went
Met three whores in a pop-up tent
They were three and we were two
So I bucked one and Timbuktu.

The children were lined up in the cafeteria of a Catholic elementary school for lunch. At the head of the table was a large pile of apples. A nun had made a note and posted it on the apple tray, 'Take only one. God is watching.'

At the other end of the table was a large pile of chocolate-chip cookies. A child had written a note, 'Take all you want. God is watching the apples.'

Peter wakes up with a huge hangover. He forces himself to open his eyes and the first thing he sees is a couple of Panadol and a glass of water on the side table. He sits down and sees his clothing in front of him, all clean and pressed. Peter looks around the room and sees that it is in perfect order, spotlessly clean. So is the rest of the house.

He takes the Panadol and notices a note on the table:

'Honey, breakfast is on the stove, I left early to go shopping. Love you.'

So he goes to the kitchen and sure enough there is a hot breakfast and the morning newspaper. His daughter is also at the table, eating.

Peter asks, 'Victoria, what happened last night?'

'Well, you came home after 3 a.m., drunk and delirious. Broke some furniture, puked in the hallway, and gave yourself a black eye when you stumbled into the door.'

'So, why is everything so clean, and why is breakfast on the table waiting for me?'

'Oh that! Well, Mum dragged you to the bedroom, and when she tried to take your pants off, you said, "Lady, leave me alone, I'm married."'

A nerd was walking on campus one day when his nerd friend rode up on an incredible shiny new bicycle. The first nerd was stunned and asked, 'Where did you get such a nice bike?'

'Well, yesterday I was walking home minding my own business when a beautiful woman rode up to me on this bike. She threw the bike to the ground, took off all her clothes and said, "Take what you want!".'

The first nerd nodded approvingly and said, 'Good choice. The clothes probably wouldn't have fitted.'

DEVIL: Why so miserable?

LARRY: What do you think? I'm in hell.

DEVIL: Hell's not so bad. We actually have a lot of fun down here. You like a drink, Larry?

LARRY: Sure, I like a drink.

DEVIL: Well you're going to love Mondays then. On Mondays that's all we do – drink. Beer, whisky, tequila, Guinness, wine coolers, diet drinks. We drink till we throw up and then we drink some more!

LARRY: Gee that sounds great.

DEVIL: You a smoker?

LARRY: You better believe it! I love smoking.

DEVIL: OK! You're going to love Tuesdays. On Tuesdays we get the finest Cuban cigars, and smoke our lungs out. If you get cancer – no problem – you're already dead, remember?

LARRY: Wow. That's awesome!

DEVIL: I bet you like to gamble.

LARRY: Why, yes, as a matter of fact, I do. Love the gambling.

DEVIL: Cause Wednesday you can gamble all you want. Blackjack, Roulette, Poker, Slots, Craps, whatever. If you go bankrupt – who cares, you're dead anyhow.

DEVIL: You into drugs?

LARRY: Are you kidding? I love drugs! You don't mean…

DEVIL: I do! Thursday is drug day. Help yourself to a great big bowl of crack. Or smack. Smoke a bong the size of a submarine. You can do all the drugs you want and if you overdose, that's OK – you're dead – so, who cares! OD as much as you like!

LARRY: Gee whiz, I never realised that hell was such a great place!

DEVIL: See, now you're getting the hang of it! Now Larry, tell me, are you gay?

LARRY: Ah, no.

DEVIL: Ooooh. Well Larry, I'm afraid you're really gonna hate Fridays.